LOS ANGELES

THEN & NOW

Thunder Bay Press
An imprint of the Baker & Taylor Publishing Group
10350 Barnes Canyon Road, San Diego, CA 92121
www.thunderbaybooks.com

Produced by Salamander Books,
an imprint of Pavilion Books Company Ltd.
1 Gower Street, London WC1E 6HD, UK

"Then and Now" is a registered trademark of Salamander Books Ltd, a division of
Pavilion Books Group.

© 2014 Salamander Books Ltd, a division of Pavilion Books Group.

Los Angeles Then and Now is a revision of the original title by Rosemary Lord,
published in 2002 by PRC Books, a division of the Pavilion Books Group.

Library of Congress Cataloging-in-Publication Data

Lord, Rosemary.
  Los Angeles then & now / Rosemary Lord. -- Revised and updated.
    pages cm
  ISBN-13: 978-1-62686-247-0
  ISBN-10: 1-62686-247-8
1. Los Angeles (Calif.)--Pictorial works. 2. Los Angeles (Calif.)--
History--Pictorial works. I. Title.
  F869.L843L66 2014
  979.4'9400222--dc23
                    2014004349

Printed in China
1 2 3 4 5 18 17 16 15 14

ACKNOWLEDGMENTS
Thanks to Kelly Wallace from the Frances Goldwyn Hollywood Library. To
Richard Adkins of Hollywood Heritage & History For Hire. Special thanks to
writer Gayle Bartos Pool for her guidance. Thanks to Dace Taube, Curator of the
University of Southern California Cultural History Library and Caroline Cole of
the Los Angeles Public Library.

And most of all—thanks to my husband Rick Cameron, my inspiration forever,
for his patience, support, and for being an infinite source of irrelevant historical
information.

PHOTO CREDITS
The publisher wishes to thank the following for kindly supplying the "then"
photography for this book:
Pages 8 (main), 12, 13, 14, 15, 17, 19, 20, 21, 23, 26, 29, 30 (inset), 37, 39, 40, 42
(inset), 45 (bottom inset), 46, 49, 51, 95, 122, 123, 131, 133, and 137 courtesy of the
Library of Congress.
Pages 8 (inset), 11, 18, 22, 28, 30, 36, 41, 42 (main), 48, 54, 56, 60, 62, 76, 80, 89,
114, 130, 134, 136, and 142 courtesy of the California Historical Society, Title
Insurance and Trust Photo Collection, Department of Special Collections,
University of Southern California.
Pages 10, 24, 38, 50, 53, 100, and 114 (inset) courtesy of Getty Images.
Page 16 courtesy of the Whittington Collection, Department of Special Collections,
University of Southern California.
Page 44, courtesy of the Hearst Newspaper Collection, Special Collections,
University of Southern California.
Pages 32, 34, 45, 47, 52, 58, 64, 83, 88, 93, 94, 106, 108, 110, 112, 113, 118, 124, 126,
128, 132, 138, and 140 courtesy of the Los Angeles Public Library.
Pages 66, 67, 68, 70, 78, 82, 84, 86, 90, 92, 96, 98, 102, 104, and 116 courtesy of the
Bruce Torrence Hollywood Historical Collection.
Pages 72 and 101 courtesy of Corbis.
Pages 120 and 121 courtesy of the Helms Bakery Archive.

All "now" images courtesy of Karl Mondon/Pavilion Image Library, with the
exception of:
Pages 11 (main), 19 (main), 21, 25, 37, 65, 99 (insets), and 101 courtesy of Vaughan
Grylls/Anova Image Library.
Pages 19 (inset), 87 (inset), 97 (insets), 123 (inset), 137 (inset), and 139 (inset)
courtesy of the Library of Congress.
Pages 11 (inset) and 13 courtesy of Simon Clay/Chrysalis Image Library.

LOS ANGELES

THEN & NOW

ROSEMARY LORD

THUNDER BAY
P·R·E·S·S

San Diego, California

LOS ANGELES

THEN & NOW INTRODUCTION

The Native Americans called Los Angeles "the Land of Smoke" because of the haze that often hangs over the basin early in the morning. They were the first to inhabit the area that is now downtown Los Angeles, which they called Yang-Na. In 1542, when Portuguese-born explorer Juan Cabrillo sailed into the harbor, he saw the smoke from the Native Americans' fires and called it "the Bay of Smokes." The early morning haze still lingers, but Los Angeles has continued to change over the decades, probably more than any other part of America.

For years, Los Angeles was just a stopping-off point between Europe and the Far East for traders of spices and silks. It was not until the Spanish, under Gaspar de Portolá's command, arrived at Yang-Na in 1769 that it was claimed and dedicated as "La Reina des los Angeles." The Spanish governor, Felipe de Neve, brought recruits from Mexico, and the forty-four settlers (which included Africans, Native Americans, Spaniards, and Mexicans) officially founded Los Angeles in 1781. Franciscan friar Junípero Serra built missions in an attempt to convert the resident Native Americans to the Christian faith.

The Native Americans were skilled craftspeople, and were used as slave labor to build the new town. In 1860 the Native American population was decimated by an outbreak of smallpox, and by 1920 only 5 percent of the original Native American population had survived. Unlike the fossilized remains of prehistoric animals trapped in time, there are scant traces of the Chumash and Tongva tribes, save a few woven baskets, stone paintings, and place-names such as Malibu, Cahuenga, and Azusa.

The first American in Los Angeles was Boston shipbuilder Joseph "Pirate Joe" Chapman in 1818. A gifted carpenter, he built the Pueblo Plaza Church. As the town spread, enterprising developers advertised: "Room for millions of immigrants, a climate for health and wealth with no cyclones or blizzards." Los Angeles was on its way to becoming a polyglot of nations. The Chinese arrived in 1870 to work as cheap labor in the gold mines and on the railroads. The gold rush also brought folks from far and wide in search of their fortunes. Many immigrants, fleeing religious persecution in Europe, came to New York and from there they made the long overland trek west in covered wagons, searching for freedom and sunshine. The majority of Los Angelenos were born elsewhere—even the palm trees that are so widespread in the area today are not indigenous to the region.

The arrival of Henry Huntingdon's Pacific Electric Railroad in 1900 marked the beginning of the trolley system that linked downtown with the ocean and midtown with the valley. In 1851 the *Los Angeles Star* was the town's first newspaper, while the rival *Los Angeles Times* was founded in 1881. Libraries, museums, schools,

and places of worship sprang up. Oil was discovered, and the cattle ranchers prospered on this "black gold."

Hollywood was created by Kansas prohibitionist Harvey Wilcox, who sold parcels of his ranch for a development to be called Figwood. However, Wilcox's wife Daeida liked the name Hollywood (a city near Chicago), and the name stuck. Little did the puritanical couple know how their innocent-sounding name would be viewed a century later. It was the Hollywood film industry that really put Los Angeles on the map, as the world escaped into their celluloid adventures and followed the often scandalous and extravagant lifestyles of the movie stars.

In 1909 bad weather in Chicago forced director Francis Boggs to complete his film in Los Angeles. *The Heart of a Race Tout* was shot in a vacant downtown Chinese laundry. However, it was New Yorkers Carl Laemmle, Cecil B. DeMille, Jesse Lasky, and Samuel Goldwyn who first built movie studios in Hollywood. DeMille's *Squaw Man* became the first feature to be filmed entirely in Hollywood. The legendary Louis B. Mayer, Jack Warner, David Selznick, and showman Sid Grauman continued the legacy, and soon the Hollywoodland sign symbolized the heart of the movie industry. Hollywood gave us films like *Gone With the Wind*, *The Grapes of Wrath*, and *It's a Wonderful Life*, and continues to enchant us today.

Today, foreign corporations own most of the film studios, and young hopefuls still flock to seek fame and fortune in Hollywood. A small train stop called Morocco became the elegant Beverly Hills area, which contains Rodeo Drive, a shopping mecca for designer fashions. The swinging 1960s saw an effort to wipe out the old and "modernize," and many beautiful buildings were torn down. Fortunately, today there is a new appreciation of the history of the "Queen of the Angels," and historical societies are busy reclaiming and restoring the old buildings.

Surviving disastrous flooding, fires, riots, and, of course, earthquakes, Los Angeles continues to attract new residents and visitors alike. This revealing book matches historic nineteenth and early twentieth century images with photographs of modern Los Angeles, showing how the multifaceted, multicultural "Dream City" has evolved while retaining its appeal as a place where dreams are born.

Olvera Street, c. 1940   *p. 10*

Pico House, 1936   *p. 14*

Union Station, c. 1940   *p. 18*

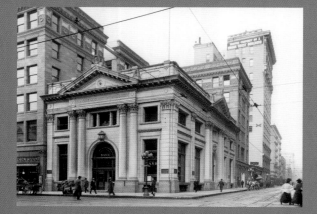

Farmers and Merchants Bank, 1908   *p. 28*

Los Angeles Times Building, c. 1940   *p. 38*

Angel's Flight, 1960   *p. 40*

Los Angeles Coliseum, c. 1935   *p. 50*

Hollywood Sign, 1935   *p. 64*

Griffith Observatory, 1935   *p. 68*

Grauman's Chinese Theatre, c. 1925   p. 88

Hollywood Memorial Park, c. 1910   p. 98

Whisky a Go Go, 1973   p. 100

Beverly Hills City Hall, c. 1931   p. 110

UCLA, 1929   p. 124

MGM-Sony Studios, c. 1925   p. 126

St. Mark's Hotel, c. 1905   p. 130

Venice Canal, c. 1935   p. 136

Santa Monica Beach, c. 1920   p. 142

OLD PLAZA CHURCH

The church is still thriving after work on it began over 200 years ago

ABOVE: Shipbuilder Joseph Chapman took four years to build Nuestra Señora la Reina de Los Angeles—Our Lady Queen of the Angels—the first church in Los Angeles, which was dedicated in 1822. The cornerstone was laid in 1814 in what was then the ruins of a small adobe mission. Until then, the Mission San Gabriel was the nearest place of worship for parishioners who walked the nine miles for Sunday services and holy days. The new church quickly became the spiritual and social center for the pueblo. The archive photo is by William Henry Jackson; it was taken between 1890 and 1900 and shows the church after it was rebuilt in 1861.

RIGHT: Our Lady's octagonal tower has been replaced by bells in the thirty years between the two archive pictures.

ABOVE: The church has been run by the Claretian Missionary Fathers since 1908 and maintains a strong role in the community. It was one of the first three Los Angeles Historic-Cultural Monuments nominated in 1962, and in the 1980s it gave sanctuary to refugees from El Salvador who had been threatened with deportation. Sparkling with fresh paint, the church is still popular for weddings, christenings, and fiestas. Once boasting the largest Roman Catholic congregation west of the Rockies, the doors are still open to immigrants and refugees in need. Over the years, the Old Plaza Church has had several face-lifts—and retrofits—but the church's role remains the same as it watches over the plaza.

c.1940

OLVERA STREET
The oldest street in Los Angeles

LEFT: Considered the oldest street in Los Angeles, Olvera Street began as a lane called Wine Street on the north side of the plaza. In 1877 it was renamed in honor of one of its residents, Agustin Olvera, the county's first judge. However, by the 1920s, the historical buildings were neglected and Olvera Street was in disrepair. In 1926 civic leader Christine Sterling, shocked to find it now a slum, began a campaign to renovate Olvera Street, enlisting her wealthy and influential friends to save this historic heart of Los Angeles.

c.1940

ABOVE: On Easter Sunday 1930, Olvera Street (paved in bricks by a local prison gang) reopened as a Mexican marketplace, and became an immediate tourist attraction. Of the four original Italian structures on the street, the Winery and the 1857 Pelanconi house remain. In 1930 the latter became La Golondrina and is the oldest restaurant in the area, while the 1818 Avila adobe (Sterling's home until her death in 1963) is the oldest existing building in the city. Today this is an exciting tourist and cultural draw with Mexican artifacts, museums, crafts, restaurants, mariachis, and Aztec dancers to entertain visitors. The Cinco de Mayo celebration, the archbishop's blessing of the animals at Easter, and the Día de los Muertos at the end of October are among the popular events held each year in the Olvera Street plaza.

ABOVE: A plaque on Olvera Street commemorates the eleven families who first settled the Pueblo de la Reina de Los Angeles in 1781.

11

1887

OLD PLAZA FIREHOUSE
The firehouse at 126 Plaza Street served that role for just thirteen years

1894

ABOVE: The building photographed in 1894 would only be used for two more years before the lease ran out. After the fire crews left, the slide pole was removed and the oval hole covered in linoleum. It was revealed again in 1950.

BELOW: The 1920 photo already shows signs of wear and tear on the building. When the state bought the building in 1950, Chinese lottery tickets—remnants of the previous occupants— were found scattered on the floor.

1920

LEFT: The firehouse at 126 Plaza Street was Los Angeles's second fire station. The debut fire crew was Volunteer 38's Engine Company No. 1—so named because there were thirty-eight men. They operated out of the plaza until 1887. Initially, there were two volunteer firefighting units in the city, but they were constantly bickering and would race each other to the fires. The new firehouse opened in September 1884, with the men housed upstairs and a brass pole for them to slide down to reach the horses that pulled the steam-driven fire engines. However, it was not until December 1885 that the city began paying its firemen.

ABOVE: Built on leased land, the fire company was forced to move out in 1897. In the ensuing years, the Plaza Firehouse deteriorated and was used as a cheap boardinghouse, a saloon, and, in 1918, as a Chinese vegetable market. The 1920 photo shows it with the entrance bricked up and a cigar store on the corner. Bought in 1950 by the State of California as part of their Historical Pueblo program, it was restored to its former glory and today serves as the Museum of Firefighting. The free museum displays firefighting equipment and historical memorabilia from the late nineteenth and early twentieth centuries.

PICO HOUSE

While the Pueblo Plaza was the hub of Los Angeles business, the Pico did a roaring trade

BELOW: In 1869 Pío Pico, the last Mexican governor of Alta California, built the Italianate Pico House in an effort to revitalize the deteriorating Pueblo Plaza. The first three-story structure there, the Pico House was an elegant hotel with luxurious baths, gas lighting, and a French restaurant. It was designed by Ezra F. Kysor, who also designed the Cathedral of St. Vibiana (see page 26). Distinguished guests attended balls, wedding receptions, and fiestas.

For several years, the Pico House was the grandest hotel in Los Angeles—until the business hub of the new city began to move south and the Pueblo Plaza fell into decline at the turn of the twentieth century.

1877

ABOVE: The Pico House in its original form without the "Old" added to the building's title. Its creator, Pío de Jesús Pico, lived to the ripe old age of ninety-three.

c.1880

ABOVE: Looking from Olvera Street toward the Pico House. Although many historians date the building to 1869, the Historic American Buildings Survey lists it as 1859.

BELOW: Floods and droughts caused many ranchers to move away from El Pueblo. The Pico House and the adjacent Merced Theatre were successful for a while, but they eventually declined along with the rest of the area. It finally passed into the hands of the State of California in 1953, and it now belongs to the El Pueblo de Los Angeles State Historic Monument. The Pico House was partially renovated in 1981 and again in 1992. After yet another careful restoration, the Pico House now hosts art and photography exhibitions, music recitals, and cultural and social events. The Pico House is frequently used as a site for films, television shows, and commercials.

c.1948

羅致菁華

CHINATOWN
Moved from its original location, the Chinese community has put down strong roots in the "new" Chinatown

16

1939

LEFT: By 1870 about 300 Chinese people were living in Old Chinatown, south of the plaza, in rundown conditions, plagued with tong wars, prostitution, and opium dens. The Chinese tenants were unceremoniously evicted from this area in 1932, as it was to be used for the new Union Station. Not permitted to live among the general population, Chinese residents were moved en masse to share Little Italy a few blocks west.

TOP LEFT: A colored postcard of the original Chinatown, circa 1905.

LEFT: The original entrance to the newly designated China City, which opened in August 1939.

ABOVE: The first "China City"—designed by American filmmakers who filmed scenes for *The Good Earth* (1937)—mysteriously burned down six months later. The new Chinatown, seen today between Broadway and Hill Street, was built in the 1930s on Chinese-owned land, with Chinese input, to provide modern amenities and comfort while retaining Chinese traditions. Chinatown quickly became a favorite with Los Angelenos and tourists alike. Served by the Gold Line of L.A.'s Metro Rail, Chinatown celebrates the Chinese New Year with the annual Golden Dragon Parade. The dozens of floats, entertainers, and marching bands attract thousands of viewers in the Asian American community. The mid-autumn Lunar Festival and the Firecracker 5K run are popular local events. Films and television shows that have been shot here include *Lethal Weapon*, *Gangster Squad*, *Rush Hour*, and *Chinatown*.

c.1940

UNION STATION
Back from the brink, Union Station bustles again in the new century

LEFT: A civic gala opened Union Station in 1939 on Alameda Street (the former site of Old Chinatown), opposite the plaza. It served the Southern Pacific, Santa Fe, and Union Pacific Railroads, and was designed by John and Donald Parkinson in a Spanish Mission style with carved ceilings, marbled floor, and a 135-foot clock tower. Before air travel became widespread, Union Station was the arrival and departure point for all Los Angelenos, including wartime GIs and movie stars such as Greta Garbo and Cary Grant.

BELOW: The station hall as photographed in 1944 by the *L.A. Daily News*. Seventy years later, the floor and wall tiling are still intact.

ABOVE: Considered the last of America's great railway stations to be built, Union Station fell on hard times when air travel became popular in the 1970s. The 1990s saw a resurgence at Union Station when the Metro Line Subway Terminal opened. Amtrak's Coastal Starlight and San Diegan emerged as the new favorite way to travel and the station's Traxx restaurant the place to eat. In 2011 the L.A. Metropolitan Transportation Authority bought Union Station for $75 million. They added several retail and dining businesses to the concourse and, in September 2013, opened the Metropolitan Lounge for business travelers. A favorite location for film and television companies, with over sixty filming sessions a year, this distinctive setting can be seen in many films, including *The Way We Were*, *Blade Runner*, and *The Dark Knight Rises*.

c.1967

SIXTH STREET VIADUCT
Los Angeles's iconic Streamline Moderne bridge

LEFT AND BELOW: The Sixth Street Viaduct was the last and grandest of the bridges and viaducts that were constructed from 1910 to 1932 as part of the City Beautiful plan of the Los Angeles Municipal Art Commission. Many of the bridges crossing the Los Angeles River were rebuilt at this time, and Sixth Street was the last to be completed. City engineer John Griffin wrote that the bridges were built to "excite favorable comment from visitors who enter and leave the city by the railways, which pass under most of these bridges" and "to raise the status of Los Angeles as an enterprising, properly developed city." There had been criticism of the industrial nature of the old iron truss bridges they replaced, and it was argued that a city's bridges were just as important a civic monument as city halls, libraries, and courthouses. The Sixth Street Viaduct was designed by Merrill Butler in the Streamline Moderne style. Each of the incised and cast-concrete columns has a different, irregular cross section.

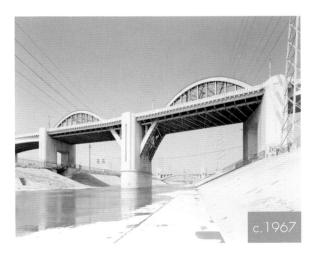

c. 1967

ABOVE: The Sixth Street Viaduct was designed to connect Los Angeles with Boyle Heights, and to facilitate this, the bridge piers were constructed at angles to allow the bridge to curve toward Boyle Heights. The Sixth, Fourth, and First Street bridges line up to cross the channelized Los Angeles River, and in 2008 the city designated all three bridges as Historic-Cultural Monuments. It's under these bridges that John Travolta raced in the movie *Grease* (1978), and Sixth Street Bridge is the only one of the twelve significant historic bridges to have ramp access to the river. Merrill Butler retired from his job as the city's bridge engineer in 1963 after forty years of service, and the bridges he designed, now seismically retrofitted, are his legacy.

VIEW FROM TEMPLE AND MAIN
The sidewalks were heaving when William Jennings Bryan came to town

1896

BELOW: Today, the site where Temple and Spring Streets met Main Street has been demolished, and the Hollywood Freeway runs underneath the now-elevated Main Street. The Bella Union Hotel was destroyed, but the Pico House and the Masonic Hall have been renovated. The main foreground seen in the archival photograph is now the site of government buildings, including the Criminal Court Building and the Hall of Records. As with most of the area after 1900, the Baker Block lost tenants and business waned. The building was purchased by Goodwill Industries in 1919, but they couldn't turn around its fortunes. The block was intended to be the site of a civic center extension and was slated for demolition. Despite attempts by the Metropolitan Garden Association to move the Baker Block and other proposals to turn it into a museum, the city purchased the Baker Block from Goodwill in 1941 and demolished it in 1942.

ABOVE: Living on borrowed time, the magnificent Baker Block just a few years before its eventual demolition. The site has not been redeveloped.

LEFT: The Baker Block in its Victorian prime.

LEFT: In 1896 the Silver Republicans had a parade for their candidate, William Jennings Bryan, and crowds gathered to cheer and enjoy the fiesta along Main Street. In the center is one of the seven 150-foot lampposts. Each of the tall masts carried three carbon-arc lamps of 3,000 candlepower. All seven installations, together with a power plant to provide the electricity, were installed by C. L. Howland in 1882. They were said to provide the illumination equivalent to a full moon. Along the right side are the famous Pico House, the 1870 Merced Theatre (Los Angeles's first theater), the Masonic Hall, and the Bella Union Hotel. The magnificent three-story Baker Block that dominates Main Street was completed around 1877, and was financed by Colonel Robert S. Baker. At the time of its completion, it was one of the most expensive structures built south of San Francisco. The grand French Second Empire building housed a variety of businesses, with stores at street level and offices and apartments above.

1929

CITY HALL
The iconic building that made it onto LAPD badges

BELOW: City Hall captured in Kodachrome in the early 1950s from North Main Street.

c.1950

LEFT: City Hall began scraping the sky just as the 1920s were coming to an end. Architects John Parkinson, John C. Austin, and Albert C. Martin Sr. designed the thirty-two-story building that, at 454 feet, stood as the tallest building in Los Angeles until 1968, when the 514-foot Union Bank Building rose up. The building is Los Angeles's third city hall building. The first, the Rocha House, stood on the northeast corner of Spring and Court Streets; the second, a grand Romanesque Revival affair, stood on Broadway between Second and Third Streets. Builders fashioned the concrete in its tower using sand from each of California's fifty-eight counties and water from the state's twenty-one historical missions. An image of City Hall has graced the Los Angeles Police Department's badges since 1940 and became a television icon when Joe Friday (played by Jack Webb) kept the city free of crime in the 1950s on the television series *Dragnet*.

RIGHT: City Hall boasts an observation level, open to the public, on the twenty-seventh floor. The Metro Red Line's Civic Center Station serves City Hall and the adjacent federal, state, and county buildings. The 1971 Sylmar earthquake, the 1987 Whittier earthquake, and the 1994 Northridge earthquake all damaged City Hall to varying degrees. Between 1998 and 2001, the building underwent a seismic retrofit that should allow it to sustain minimal damage and remain functional in the event of a magnitude 8.2 earthquake. Making the building as safe as possible is nothing new. The building's original architects separated each floor with flexible compression zones that mimic the human spine in their ability to twist, shake, and return to their original form. Government functions have grown over the years to necessitate the building of a sixteen-story City Hall East and an eight-story City Hall South.

c.1900

CATHEDRAL OF ST. VIBIANA
The cathedral survived an archdiocese that wanted it torn down

ABOVE: The Cathedral of St. Vibiana, seat of the Los Angeles Archdiocese, was completed in 1876 when Los Angeles's population reached 5,500—3,000 of whom were Catholics. Designed by Ezra Kysor, it was modeled after a Baroque church in Barcelona, on land donated by Amiel Cavalier at a cost of $80,000— and seats well over a thousand. Inside, preserved in a marble sarcophagus, are the relics of the early Christian martyr St. Vibiana.

1960

ABOVE: The Cathedral of St. Vibiana was severely damaged by earthquakes in 1971 and 1994. The neglected cathedral was closed in 1995. The archdiocese proposed St. Vibiana's be torn down and a new cathedral built. After much public protest, St. Vibiana's was saved and bought by developer Tom Gilmore

LEFT: The cathedral at Second and Main has seen buildings come and go on either side of it, but has outlasted them all.

for use as a performing arts center. The ultramodern Cathedral of Our Lady of the Angels was built on the corner of Temple and Grand Avenue at a cost said to be in excess of $200 million—$6 million was spent carefully restoring the newly named Vibiana, which is a thriving cultural center, hosting art exhibits, fashion shows, and conferences. The gilded foyer and forty-five-foot-high main hall—complete with baroque columns, century-old marble, and a grand stage—are complemented with high-tech sound and lighting systems.

FARMERS AND MERCHANTS BANK

The first incorporated bank in Los Angeles, it is the last surviving example of a Beaux Arts bank

LEFT AND RIGHT: The Farmers and Merchants Bank, founded by Isaias Hellman in 1871, was the first incorporated bank in Los Angeles. Photographed in 1908, the Farmers and Merchants Bank on the corner of Main and Fourth Streets was built in 1905 and was designed by the firm of Morgan and Wells. Hellman, a real-estate speculator, merchant, and banker, remained president of the bank until his death in 1920.

BELOW: The last surviving example of a Beaux Arts banking temple, the Farmers and Merchants Bank operated as a bank until its closure in the late 1980s. This Historic-Cultural Monument was restored to its former elegance. The original banking room, loggia, and central skylight remain, with luxurious loft apartments, art studios, galleries, and banquet facilities. The Romanesque facade and interior are frequently used for filming as well as for social events.

c.1925

c.1933

BROADWAY FROM OLYMPIC

Home to the Broadway Theater District

LEFT: Broadway originally started out as a dirt road named Eternity Street, so called because it led to a cemetery. Renamed in 1890, Broadway was the main entertainment street in downtown Los Angeles until the 1960s. Seen here in 1928, it boasted the most vaudeville and movie palaces in the country. The United Artists Theatre opened on December 26, 1927, with *My Best Girl*, starring theater owner Mary Pickford. Pickford and her husband Douglas Fairbanks, who co-owned the United Artists Theatre, showed their lavish films here. The Eastern Columbia Building at 849 South Broadway rivals City Hall as one of the finest surviving examples of Art Deco architecture in the city. Just across the street from the Orpheum Theatre, it was designed by Claud Beelman and opened on September 12, 1930. It served as the new headquarters of the Eastern Outfitting Company and the Columbia Outfitting Company, furniture and clothing stores.

BELOW: The thirteen-story Eastern Outfitting Company Building, which has been called "the best extant example of a ziggurat skyscraper clad in polychrome terra-cotta."

c.1975

RIGHT: As people and businesses moved west, Broadway was gradually abandoned and neglected. A largely immigrant population of vendors took over the elaborate old theaters of the 1920s. The sumptuous movie palaces became discount shops and flea markets. The Spanish Gothic–style United Artists Theatre became Gene Scott's University Cathedral with a "Jesus Saves" sign overhead—until 2011. New owners renovated the entire building and opened the Ace Hotel in January 2014. They refurbished the United Artists Theatre, which is used for special events and rented out for filming. This was part of the resurgence of downtown Los Angeles and the ten-year "Bringing Back Broadway" plan. With the conversion of many old buildings to loft apartments, the downtown area now had over 45,000 more local inhabitants. Many of the young residents supported the restorations and have introduced new, creative art and performance venues, merging the two worlds. This is bringing people back not just to the theaters but to the streets of downtown Los Angeles, the home to the largest surviving group of pre–World War II theaters. The Eastern Building was listed as a Los Angeles Historic-Cultural Monument in 1985.

BELOW: The Eastern Lofts as they look today, with the turquoise terra-cotta catching the sun's low rays.

1931

LOS ANGELES THEATRE

Built in record time with no expense spared

LEFT: The Los Angeles Theatre was built in 1931 for the opening of Charlie Chaplin's film *City Lights*. With only thirty days to go before the scheduled premiere—the entire theater was constructed off-site—the structure was swung in and slotted between the existing buildings. The lavish French Baroque interior had a central staircase and gold brocade drapes more befitting an opera house, and it cost more than a million dollars. Chaplin helped fund it to get his perfect premiere venue.

ABOVE: Built at the start of the Great Depression, it was the last extravagant movie palace in Los Angeles. The opulent French Baroque interior had touches of the Hall of Mirrors in Versailles. The crystal fountain can be seen at the head of the grand staircase.

RIGHT: With the hoopla of jazzy premieres behind it, the Los Angeles Theatre, like many others, fell into disrepair. After years of being empty, it survived by showing Mexican films and was then closed to the public. It continues to be used for special events and as a filming location—including *Charlie's Angels*, *The Jay Leno Show*, and *Mad Men*. The Los Angeles Conservancy has sponsored showings of classic films here and at other famous Broadway movie theaters for the "Last Remaining Seats" events as part of the program to revive and restore these dream palaces.

1927

TOWER THEATER

The first downtown theater to welcome in the talkies

LEFT: Previously the site of the 900-seat Hyman Theatre (later renamed the Garrick Theatre) built in 1911, the Tower Theater opened its doors in 1927. It was architect S. Charles Lee's first theater design. Lee was just twenty-eight at the time, but would go on to design around 400 theaters. Seating 1,000 on a tiny site, it was built in powerful Baroque style with innovative French, Spanish, Moorish, and Italian elements all executed in terra-cotta. The theater was equipped with a Wurlitzer 2 manual ten-rank theater organ. The very top of the clock tower was removed after the 1932 Jalisco earthquake. This was the first downtown theater to play "talkies."

ABOVE: Like many other theaters on Broadway, the Tower Theater was abandoned for many years. It remained mostly intact, but rundown, with its famous tower still standing. The lobby was rented to vendors and the theater was used for filming in *The Mambo Kings*, *Mulholland Drive*, *Fight Club*, and *The Prestige*, among others. The Living Faith Evangelical Church rented the venue until the Delijani family bought the Tower and three other classic theaters. The Delijanis' multimillion-dollar renovation will turn the Tower Theater into a high-tech concert venue, coffeehouse, and nightclub.

1927

MAYAN THEATRE
Opened as a conventional theater, the Mayan soon started showing movies

ABOVE AND RIGHT: The Belasco and Mayan Theatres were designed by the architectural firm of Morgan, Walls, and Clements and opened as conventional theaters in 1926 and 1927, respectively. The owners were hoping to establish a new theater district west of Broadway with the Mayan at 1040 South Hill and the Belasco at 1050 South Hill. The Belasco's opening production was the comedy *Gentlemen Prefer Blondes* (with an advertisement still visible on the side of the building until it was repainted in 2006) while the Mayan opened with the musical comedy *Oh Kay!* starring Elsie Janis. By 1929 the Mayan had started showing movies and in 1931 it was being billed as Grauman's Mayan.

1927

ABOVE AND ABOVE LEFT: Legitimate theater wasn't abandoned at the Mayan, and as part of the WPA Federal Theater Project in the 1930s it put on shows such as *Follow the Parade* and *Volpone*. It switched between stage shows and Spanish-language films in the 1940s and 1950s. Duke Ellington played 101 shows to an unsegregated audience here starting in 1941, a time when audiences were segregated downtown. The 1960s and 1970s proved to be hard times, and in the early 1970s it started to show adult movies (some of which were shot in the basement). In 1977 the auditorium was split into three screens—still showing adult movies—until 1990, when the venue became the Mayan nightclub, which it remains today. The neighboring Belasco was closed in 1952 and subsequently used as a community church. There were plans to convert it into a nightclub, but after a $10 million renovation it reopened as a theater in 2011.

c.1940

LOS ANGELES TIMES BUILDING
A gold medal winner at the 1937 Paris Exposition

ABOVE: The *Los Angeles Times* newspaper was first published December 4, 1881, in a small brick building at Temple and New High Street. On October 1, 1910, the building was dynamited by union activists, destroying the building, killing twenty-one people, and injuring many. Owner Harrison Gray Otis had been fighting to keep the paper an "open shop" for workers. The paper was then run from a branch office at 531 South Spring Street. Otis died in 1917 and Harry Chandler, his son-in-law, became the second publisher of the *Times*. The new Art Deco Los Angeles Times Building opened in 1935 on the corner of First and Spring Streets. At the time, it was the largest building on the West Coast used entirely for newspaper publishing. Designed by Gordon B. Kaufman, it won a gold medal at the 1937 Paris Exposition for its modern architectural style. The Globe Lobby has ten-foot-high murals painted by Hugo Ballin in 1934.

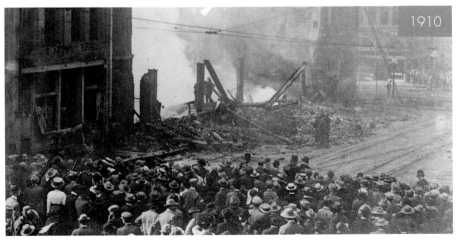

1910

ABOVE: In 1989, following the closure of rival paper the *Herald-Examiner*, the *Times* hired many *Herald* staffers, bought their subscription list, and took over several *Herald* features. The following year, the *Times'* circulation reached an all-time high. In June 2002, the *Times* merged with the *Chicago Tribune* and became part of a large media group. The lobby has an historical exhibit showcasing the first 100 years of the *Times*. Free tours of the building and printing facility are offered to the public.

LEFT: The shell of the Los Angeles Times Building at First and Broadway in 1910. Sixteen sticks of dynamite were packed into a suitcase and were due to go off at 4:00 a.m., when the building would be empty. Instead, the bomb detonated just after 1:00 a.m., with a late-night team still producing an extra edition for the Vanderbilt Cup. The explosion set off a natural gas main and the ensuing fire collapsed the building. The leadership of the Iron Workers Union, who had been responsible for the bombing, were involved in protracted court battles to establish who should be punished for the crime.

1960

ANGEL'S FLIGHT
The world's shortest railroad is back in business

BELOW: The Third Street tunnel was completed in 1901, allowing traffic to pass through Bunker Hill. It was subsequently replicated by the Second Street tunnel, which was begun in 1916 and opened in 1924, to ease congestion on the older tunnel.

c.1925

LEFT: In 1901 J. W. Eddy built the Los Angeles Incline Railway at Third and Hill Streets to connect downtown with the upper-class residential area of Bunker Hill. Soon renamed Angel's Flight and dubbed "the world's shortest railroad," its two counterbalancing white cars, Sinai and Olivet (named after biblical mountains), descended and ascended the hill for one penny each way until 1953, when the price was raised to a nickel for a round-trip. The archway was added in 1908, and in 1930 the cars were painted orange and black.

ABOVE: By the 1960s, Bunker Hill had become rundown and was replaced with office buildings and a senior citizens' housing complex. Angel's Flight was dismantled and stored. Thirty years later, in 1996, the new Angel's Flight was installed just half a block south of the original location. At twenty-five cents a ride, the funicular was highly popular until a fatal accident occurred in February 2001 and it was closed for repair. Angel's Flight reopened in 2010 at fifty cents a ride and has been running safely ever since.

c.1885

STATE NORMAL SCHOOL / L.A. PUBLIC LIBRARY

A unique building, the 1926 library displays many architectural styles

ABOVE: In the 1880s, the growing population of Los Angeles needed a place of learning, and in 1882 the State Normal School opened and welcomed its first students, most of whom were women. By 1914 the school had moved to a larger facility on Vermont Avenue. It continued to grow, and in 1919 the newly named Southern Branch of the University of Los Angeles (later UCLA) began a search for a larger site, which was eventually found in Westwood. The original school site at Fifth and Grand became the home of the Los Angeles Public Library.

c.1905

1971

FAR LEFT: The main library building was originally based in City Hall.

LEFT: The Los Angeles Public Library is a unique building with influences from the Beaux Arts, Art Deco, and Mission styles. The building has many examples of stylized Egyptian sculpture and wall paintings.

ABOVE: The new Central Library Building, specially designed by Bertram Goodhue, opened in 1926 with numerous entrances, tide pools, and lawns. These were gradually reduced with the growth of downtown and the need for parking space. After two arson fires in the 1980s, the library was restored at a cost of $125 million and expanded with four stories above and four stories and parking underground, as well as a stunning rear atrium. The archives include over three million historic photographs and a 2012 donation of over a million maps. The library facade looks just as it did in 1926.

c.1928

BILTMORE HOTEL
An early home for the Academy Awards ceremony

1943

1960

LEFT: At 506 South Grand Avenue, the Biltmore Hotel towers over Pershing Square. Designed by Schultze and Weaver, the $10 million Biltmore opened on October 1, 1923, with 1,500 rooms. It was the largest hotel west of Chicago at the time, an exotic mixture of architectural styles. Italian artist Giovanni Smeraldi, known for his work in the Vatican and the White House, was employed to produce frescoes on the ceilings of the main Galleria and the Crystal Ballroom, and a grand Spanish Baroque Revival bronze doorway was installed, complete with an astrological clock. The Academy of Motion Picture Arts and Sciences was founded at a lunch in the Crystal Ballroom in May 1927. Legend has it that MGM art director Cedric Gibbons sketched the design for the Oscar statue on a linen Biltmore napkin.

BELOW: Foreign royalty and numerous U.S. presidents have slept here. Everything from Academy Award dinners to John F. Kennedy's Democratic Convention have been held here, and the Beatles were once helicoptered onto the hotel roof and hid here for days. With the resurgence of Pershing Square, the hotel—now the Millennium Biltmore—has also had a multimillion-dollar face-lift. In October 2013, they held a star-studded ninetieth anniversary celebration. The hotel continues to be a popular location for films and TV shows such as *Mad Men* and *Glee*. Meanwhile, the adjacent Pershing Square has been upgraded with a concert stage, fountains, puppet shows, a miniature train ride, a seasonal ice rink, numerous modern art exhibits, and public seating areas.

SPANISH-AMERICAN WAR MONUMENT, PERSHING SQUARE

There is tragedy behind the monument for soldiers who never got to fight

c.1915

LEFT: The corner of Pershing Square circa 1920 shows the monument to California's twenty Spanish-American War dead and the Seventh California Infantry, which was erected in 1900. The figure was said to be modeled on war veteran Charlie Hammond of San Francisco, and is believed to be the oldest public work of art in Los Angeles. Tragically, none of the soldiers got to fight overseas, either in Cuba, the Philippines, or Puerto Rico. They all died of illnesses contracted while waiting to be deployed from San Francisco. Across Central Park and to the right of the archive photo is the Clune's Auditorium. It started as the Temple Auditorium, a large venue for the Temple Baptist Church with two smaller halls and a nine-story office block, designed by Charles E. Whittlesey. A grand foyer ran along the Olive Street side of the building with eighty-four feet of exit doors, allowing the auditorium to be emptied in under three minutes. Theatrical productions ran alongside religious services until 1914, when the auditorium was leased by local impresario William "Billy" Clune. He converted the 2,700-seat venue into the largest movie palace west of New York. When Clune showed D. W. Griffith's epic *Birth of a Nation*, he hired a full orchestra to play the score of the movie.

BELOW: Clune's Auditorium is seen on the left.

c.1915

BELOW: Pershing Square has been altered and remodeled many times since 1920, and the monument has lost its pedestal and has been moved. It now sits next to one of the many concrete spheres introduced to the landscaping. The Los Angeles City Council declared the Spanish-American War monument a Historic-Cultural Monument in 1990. Clune's tenure of his "Theatre Beautiful," as the auditorium was sometimes known, ended in 1920 when the lease ran out. In 1921 the Los Angeles Philharmonic Orchestra moved in and was joined several years later by the Los Angeles Civic Light Opera. Both remained in the auditorium until the Los Angeles Music Center was built for them in 1965. It continued in use as a church, although the original interior—and its subsequent Art Deco remodeling—was hidden by false walls and ceilings. A plan to restore it in the 1980s never materialized. It was demolished in 1985 to become part of an office development.

1910

SHRINE AUDITORIUM
Still owned by the Shriners

48

LEFT: The original Shrine Auditorium, built in 1906, was a triumph of architecture and engineering. The auditorium, seen here in 1910, caught fire on January 11, 1920, and was destroyed in thirty minutes. When the architects built the current Shrine Auditorium in 1926, they were able to make it earthquake-proof and fire-resistant. John C. Austin's ornate Moorish design was based on the Arabian-Egyptian Masonic symbolism.

1929

ABOVE AND LEFT: The 12,000-square-foot stage and a seating capacity of 6,300 make this a popular venue for award shows. The Academy Awards ceremony first came to the Shrine Auditorium in 1947 and returned—temporarily—in the late 1980s. The Bolshoi Ballet, Mikhail Baryshnikov, Bruce Springsteen, and Michael Jackson have performed here, and *King Kong* was filmed here. The Grammy Awards, MTV Awards, Comic Relief, *Soul Train*, and the Screen Actors Guild Awards have all found a home at this "West Coast Taj Mahal," with its Pavilion Ballroom, which has room for 5,200 diners and 7,500 dancers. In 2013 the entertainment company Goldenvoice took over management of the Shrine Auditorium, but it is still owned by Al Malaikah Auditorium Company—a division of the Shriners, a charitable organization.

TOP LEFT: A Shrine convention parade tours around the Los Angeles Coliseum in June 1929. The banner held up behind the performing band reads "Smile with Nile."

LOS ANGELES COLISEUM
The stadium with a unique Olympic pedigree

c.1935

LEFT AND RIGHT: Commissioned in 1921 to honor veterans of World War I, the Los Angeles Memorial Coliseum opened in 1923. At a cost of just under $1 million, the venue offered a seating capacity of 75,144. The first football game held in the stadium took place on October 6, 1923, when the University of Southern California beat Pomona College, 23–7. By 1930 Los Angeles had emerged onto the world stage and earned the honor of hosting the 1932 Olympic Games. The city scrambled to accommodate everyone, expanding the Coliseum's seating to 101,574. Fifty-two years later, the stadium did it again, hosting the 1984 Olympics. The Olympic cauldron torch remains on site, as do other Olympic symbols and statues. At the Coliseum's Court of Honor, visitors can learn about Olympic history through plaques and a full list of the 1932 and 1984 gold medalists.

c.1923

RIGHT: The State of California, Los Angeles County, and the City of Los Angeles jointly own the Los Angeles Memorial Coliseum, located in today's University Park neighborhood. It is the only stadium in the world to have hosted two Olympic Games, as well as the only Olympic stadium to have also hosted the Super Bowl and the World Series. The Coliseum became a National Historic Landmark on July 27, 1984, the day before the opening ceremony of the 1984 Olympics. In dramatic Hollywood fashion, the Olympic cauldron still sees regular use. In solidarity, the torch is lit during Olympics held in other cities. When tragedy strikes, the torch may stay lit for days, as it did after the 1986 space shuttle *Challenger* disaster. The torch burned for a full week after the September 11, 2001, terrorist attacks, and again in honor of President Ronald Reagan after his passing in 2004. The Los Angeles Memorial Sports Arena (far right) was built next to the Coliseum; it opened on July 4, 1959.

1963

DODGER STADIUM
Chavez Ravine was cleared for the Dodgers' new stadium

ABOVE: In the 1940s, Chavez Ravine was a poor, mostly Mexican American community in Sulfir Canyon. Named for Julian Chavez, a nineteenth-century city councilman, the canyon was home to mainly Hispanic families. The Los Angeles City Housing Authority earmarked Chavez Ravine's 300-plus acres as a prime location for redevelopment. In July 1950, all residents of Chavez Ravine received letters from the city telling them that they would have to sell their homes. Construction of Dodger Stadium began nine years later, and the Los Angeles Dodgers played their first game in Chavez Ravine in 1962. The parking lot offers room for 16,000 cars in twenty-one terraced lots. Since its opening, Dodger Stadium has welcomed an average of 2.8 million fans per season. Its seating capacity of 56,000 is one of the largest in Major League Baseball.

ABOVE: Dodgers pitcher Sandy Koufax in action against the Milwaukee Braves at Dodger Stadium in August 1963.

ABOVE: The 1978 season saw Dodger Stadium become the first ballpark to host more than three million fans in a season. Pope John Paul II celebrated Mass at Dodger Stadium on September 16, 1987. Entertainers from around the world have performed here, including the Rolling Stones, the Beatles, the Bee Gees, Michael Jackson, U2, and Bruce Springsteen. After the 1995 season, a new turf known as Prescription Athletic Turf was installed. It uses state-of-the-art technology to manage field moisture through controlled drainage and irrigation. By the 2000 season, the Dodgers had added new field-level seats down the foul lines and a new expanded dugout section, among other improvements. In 2003 a new scoreboard and a "DodgerVision" video board were added. After the 2005 season, all the seats within the primary seating bowl were replaced with seats that returned the stadium's look to its original 1962 color palette of yellow, light orange, turquoise, and sky blue.

c.1940

AMBASSADOR HOTEL
When Hollywood was in its heyday, the Ambassador was swinging

ABOVE: When the sprawling 400-room, Italian-style Ambassador Hotel opened on Wilshire Boulevard in 1921, it quickly became the place to be seen. By April 21, the Grand Ballroom had been converted into a nightclub that became world famous: Cocoanut Grove, otherwise known as the "Playground to the Stars." Guests enjoyed a tropical grove of several hundred fake palm trees (left over from the filming of Rudolph Valentino's *The Sheik*) with fake monkeys climbing them. The tables and chairs were bamboo and wicker. This was the height of exotic glamour in the 1920s, and the stars lined up to attend and play. Charlie Chaplin entertained, Howard Hughes danced the rumba, Judy Garland sang, and Joan Crawford and Carole Lombard were said to have competed for dance trophies here. Pola Negri would walk her pet cheetah on the manicured grounds of the hotel. During the 1930s, six Academy Awards ceremonies and the first Golden Globe Awards dinner were held at the Cocoanut Grove.

RIGHT: The Ambassador's nightclub, the Cocoanut Grove, through its links to Hollywood stars, became more famous than the hotel itself.

c.1965

FEW WILL HAVE THE GREATNESS TO BEND
HISTORY; BUT EACH OF US CAN WORK TO
CHANGE A SMALL PORTION OF EVENTS,
AND IN THE TOTAL OF ALL THOSE ACTS
WILL BE WRITTEN THE HISTORY OF THIS
GENERATION... IT IS FROM NUMBERLESS
DIVERSE ACTS OF COURAGE AND BELIEF
THAT HUMAN HISTORY IS THUS SHAPED.

2003

ABOVE: Seen in a mothballed state in 2003, the Ambassador had many futures planned out for it, but in the end fell victim to the wrecking ball.

ABOVE: Having just secured the California Democratic presidential primary on June 5, 1968, Senator Robert F. Kennedy was assassinated as he passed through the kitchen area of the hotel by Palestinian gunman Sirhan Sirhan. The tragedy helped accelerate the hotel's demise, along with the slide of the neighborhood. Despite a mid-1970s renovation overseen by Sammy Davis Jr., the hotel was closed in 1989. It was used as a backdrop to many films as it slowly declined over the next twenty years. It featured in *Pretty Woman*, *L.A. Story*, *The Wedding Singer*, *Apollo 13*, *Beaches*, *Scream 2*, *Catch Me If You Can*, *The Mask*, *Forrest Gump*, and *Fear and Loathing in Las Vegas*. Perhaps the greatest memorial to the Ambassador Hotel was the movie *The Thirteenth Floor*, which transformed it back to 1937 Los Angeles. From 2004 to 2005, it became the subject of a legal tussle between the Los Angeles Unified School District, which wanted to build a school on the site, and preservationists who wanted the hotel restored. The Robert F. Kennedy Community Schools were eventually built on the site and opened in 2009 and 2010.

c.1940

BULLOCKS WILSHIRE
The Art Deco department store was beautifully preserved by the Southwestern University School of Law

LEFT: Inspired by new designs at the Paris Exposition, John Bullock— along with John and Donald Parkinson—created the magnificent Art Deco Bullocks Wilshire department store building in 1929 as a mecca for well-heeled shoppers. With its distinctive copper-clad tower and glazed terra-cotta tile, the main entrance was at the rear, complete with uniformed parking valets. Greta Garbo, Marlene Dietrich, John Wayne, Clark Gable, and Barbara Stanwyck were devoted patrons, and Cary Grant filmed *Topper* here in 1930. Angela Lansbury worked in the store as a teenager and, many years later, came back to film an episode of *Murder, She Wrote*.

ABOVE: Shoppers moved west as new malls sprang up, and Bullocks Wilshire fell into decline. But the top-floor tearoom, famous for its coconut cream pie and fashion shows, was popular to the end. When the store closed in 1996, it was bought by the Southwestern University School of Law and restored to its former splendor. Southwestern won awards for the preservation and restoration. The famous tearoom is now a cafeteria and study hall, but can be rented for private events. It is open to the public during summer break only, on the school's annual Tea and Tour Day. The building continues to be used for filming when school is not in session. *Ghostbusters*, *Dunston Checks In*, and *The Aviator* have all been filmed here.

WILSHIRE BOULEVARD

An artery boasting almost every architectural style

LEFT: Wilshire Boulevard is one of the city's principal roads. It was named for Ohio native Henry Gaylord Wilshire, who made—and lost—fortunes in real estate, farming, and gold mining. In the 1890s, Wilshire cleared out a path in his barley field and initiated what was to become his eponymous street. The artery connects five of the city's major business districts with Beverly Hills and Santa Monica. Along its sixteen miles, through three cities from downtown Los Angeles to the ocean, Wilshire Boulevard is lined with buildings representing virtually every major architectural style of the twentieth century. Many of the city's skyscrapers are along Wilshire; one of the oldest and tallest is known simply as One Wilshire. In this 1928 photo, the Wilshire Boulevard Christian Church appears at the right, with the Brown Derby restaurant just nudging into the frame below it. Billboards took advantage of heavy traffic to promote movies like *Four Sons*, a silent drama directed and produced by John Ford.

1928

1955

RIGHT: The Brown Derby restaurant is a memory, but the Wilshire Christian Church still presides over the scene, dwarfed by condos and office towers. The church's congregation merged with two others in 1940 and dropped the "Boulevard" from its name. The Wilshire Christian Church was sold in 2013 to the Oasis Church, a Christian-based multidenominational organization with multifaith services and outreach programs. The former worshippers at the church now meet in a location downtown. The building stands at the corner of South Normandie Avenue, just across the street from the former site of the Ambassador Hotel. The area has a diverse residential population of about 130,000 and there is a large concentration of Korean-owned businesses in the area.

LEFT: The last vestiges of Victorian Los Angeles clung on till the postwar years on Wilshire Boulevard, so while there are representatives of every building style from the twentieth century, those of the nineteenth have all but disappeared.

c.1933

WILSHIRE TEMPLE
The second grand temple building created in the city

ABOVE: In 1862 B'nai B'rith was the first Jewish congregation in Los Angeles. Ten years later, they built their first temple on Fort Street, now Broadway. As membership increased, they moved to this imposing Byzantine-inspired temple on Wilshire Boulevard in 1929. The Wilshire Temple, designed by the firm of Edelman, Norton, and Allison, is one of the largest, most influential reform synagogues. It was known as the "Temple of the Stars" because Al Jolson, Jack Benny, the Warner brothers, Irving Thalberg, and other celebrities attended temple here.

c.1880

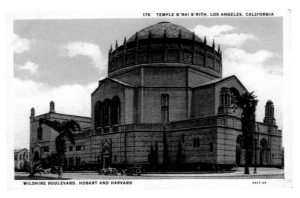

176 TEMPLE B'NAI B'RITH, LOS ANGELES, CALIFORNIA

WILSHIRE BOULEVARD, HOBART AND HARVARD 4927-29

ABOVE: A 1930s postcard of the new B'nai B'rith.

LEFT: The original B'nai B'rith temple on Fort Street (now Broadway) between Second and Third Streets. The Hebrew Benevolent Society was formed in 1854 with the aim of creating a Jewish cemetery in the city.

ABOVE: In 1984 the Byzantine Revival building was placed on the National Register of Historic Places as an acknowledgment of its architectural significance. In 1999 the Dalai Lama addressed the American Buddhist Congress at the temple. Fittingly, Canadian poet and songwriter Leonard Cohen, who embraces both Judaism and Buddhism, played a Shabbat service here in November 2012. Today, older Hollywood stalwarts remain loyal to the temple, supporting the many charitable endeavors. The 2,400-family temple congregation created a $150 million fund to restore the building because—like other buildings of its years—the temple was showing its age. The plans include extending the Erika J. Glazer Family Campus and building a new school, parking structure, gardens, and the Karsh Family Social Service Center.

BROWN DERBY RESTAURANT

It was slated for demolition, reprieved, then moved

ABOVE: An icon that was synonymous with the golden age of Hollywood, the Brown Derby was a chain started by Robert Cobb and Herbert Somborn (Gloria Swanson's husband), who opened their first restaurant on 3377 Wilshire Boulevard in 1926. The Brown Derby is considered an example of the representational architecture movement popular in Southern California during the 1920s and 1930s. The whimsical hat design was intended to catch the attention of motorists speeding by. A second Brown Derby was opened at 1628 North Vine Street in 1928, in Cecil B. DeMille's building. In the heart of Hollywood, it soon attracted studio workers and movie stars such as Clark Gable, Loretta Young, John Barrymore, and George Raft. An artist offered to sketch the famous patrons in return for food—and so the "Wall of Famous Caricatures" began.

1939

ABOVE: The iconic hat-shaped Brown Derby was saved from the wrecking ball when one of the waitresses alerted preservationists with just hours to spare. Although the restaurant closed, this original structure was moved to the rear of a two-story Korean mall up the street. The Vine Street Brown Derby closed in 1985 and mysteriously burned down in 1988. Memories of the restaurant, along with the famous Cobb salad—named after Robert Cobb—live on. The Brown Derby has since made licensing agreements with Walt Disney, Disney World, and the MGM Hotel in Las Vegas to build replicas of the Brown Derby restaurants at their facilities.

LEFT: The Brown Derby as it looked thirteen years after its opening. Permanent floodlights were subsequently added in front of the building for special events. Today, the dome still exists, but it has been moved to the back of the shopping mall and painted pink.

1935

THE HOLLYWOOD SIGN
The sign fell rapidly into decline once maintenance ceased in 1939

LEFT: By the time this picture was taken in 1935, the Hollywoodland sign had been gracing Mount Lee in the Santa Monica Mountains for thirteen years. The original Hollywoodland sign was erected in 1923 by developers as an advertising gimmick. The letters were fifty feet tall and thirty feet wide, and were made of white-painted metal squares studded with 4,000 twenty-watt bulbs; the sign cost $21,000 to build. The sign was maintained by a caretaker who lived in a small house behind the sign. A thirty-five-foot white-painted metal circle (seen as a small white dot from miles away) was put 200 feet below as an eye-catcher. An inspiration to many, the Hollywoodland sign spelled shattered dreams to actress Peg Entwhistle, who jumped from the letter H to her death fifty feet below in 1932. In the 1940s, Albert Kothe, the man entrusted with caring for the sign, got drunk, swerved off the road, and collided with the same H in his Model A Ford.

ABOVE: In 1939 maintenance ceased and 4,000 lightbulbs were stolen by vandals. Developers donated the sign to the city, which decided to restore just the "Hollywood" without the "land." During the 1960s, the Hollywood Kiwanis Club raised enough money to repair the sign. But soon after Kiwanis spent the last of their funds, one of the Os crumbled. In 1978 shock rocker Alice Cooper spearheaded a public campaign to restore the landmark when he donated $27,000 to replace the missing O. Hugh Hefner and Andy Williams were among other celebrities donating money to save the sign. The sign is now maintained by the Hollywood Sign Trust, ensuring the preservation of this Hollywood symbol. Residents living close to the sign complain about the increasing number of tourists and tour buses seeking close access to the summit, and post placards reading "Tourists Go Away."

BEACHWOOD GATES
The entrance to Hollywoodland

BELOW: Developer Albert Beach paved the way to the Hollywood Hills with a road he named after himself: Beachwood Drive. In 1923 the director of Pacific Electric Railway, M. H. Sherman, joined Harry Chandler, Tracey Shoults, and developer S. H. Woodruff and formed the Hollywoodland Tract Realty with an office at the Hollywoodland entrance. They built two stone towers on either side and planned to gate the community with a guard on night duty—but the gate and the guard never materialized.

1924

c.1924

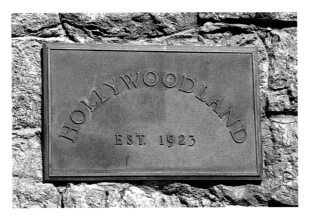

ABOVE: The developers organized bus tours of their new estate to show prospective buyers the variety of plots on offer.

ABOVE: The plaque on the Beachwood Gates at the entrance to Hollywoodland.

1935

GRIFFITH OBSERVATORY

The Welsh-born benefactor never got to see his great gift to the city

ABOVE AND ABOVE RIGHT: Colonel Griffith J. Griffith donated 3,015 acres to the City of Los Angeles in 1896 for the creation of a "great park." After making a fortune in Mexican silver mines, Griffith had invested in Southern California real estate. He visited the world's largest telescope at the new research observatory established at Mount Wilson, north of Los Angeles, in 1904. The telescope so impressed him that, in 1912, Griffith offered Los Angeles $100,000 to build an observatory atop Mount Hollywood. Griffith's plan included an astronomical telescope open to free viewing, a hall of science, and an auditorium. The Griffith Observatory has graced the south-facing slope of Mount Hollywood in Griffith Park since 1935, when these photographs were taken. Colonel Griffith died in 1919, fourteen years before construction on the site began.

1935

BELOW: During World War II, a large air-raid siren was set up next door and squadrons of naval aviators learned to navigate by the stars in the planetarium. Cosmologist Fritz Zwicky, who discovered dark matter, neutron stars, and supernovas, used the telescope for his research several times in the 1950s. The 1980s and 1990s brought unprecedented crowds to the Griffith Observatory, with attendance reaching an annual average of about two million visitors. The copper domes of the observatory were shined up to a "penny finish" in 1984, a year before the celebration of the building's fiftieth anniversary. Major astronomical events such as Halley's comet in 1986 and the impact of the comet Shoemaker-Levy 9 with Jupiter in 1994 raised the observatory's profile even further. A 1990 master plan for restoration and expansion closed the observatory for four years. In 2006 the Griffith Observatory reopened to the public after undergoing a complete renovation.

c.1920

LASKY-DEMILLE BARN / CHASE BANK

When DeMille and Lasky rented a barn in an orange grove, it was a seminal moment in Hollywood history

ABOVE: In New York in 1913, Jesse Lasky formed the Lasky Feature Play Company with director Cecil B. DeMille. After finding Arizona unsuitable for filming a Western, they continued on to Hollywood. DeMille and Lasky rented a horse barn in the middle of an orange grove, on the southeast corner of Vine Street and Selma Avenue, just above Sunset, for their studio. In 1914 their film *The Squaw Man* became the first full-length feature film made in Hollywood. In 1925 Lasky's Feature Play Company merged with Adolph Zukor's Famous Players Films to form the Famous Players–Lasky Corporation.

RIGHT: In 1926 the company moved this barn-studio to the back lot of the United Studios on Marathon and Van Ness. In 1938 NBC Radio Studios was built on Vine Street between Sunset and Selma. Today, a multipurpose building and a Chase Bank occupy the site. The Pioneers of Radio Museum remains in the basement. United Studios was renamed Paramount-Famous-Lasky in 1927 and eventually became Paramount Studios. The original horse barn used for *The Squaw Man* was stored at Paramount until 1979, when it was moved to Highland Avenue, opposite the Hollywood Bowl, and became the Hollywood Heritage Museum.

1944

NBC BUILDING / CHASE BANK
Successor to the Lasky-DeMille barn

1944

BELOW: The days of visitors to Radio City's touring studios, giant control rooms, and other behind-the-scenes features of radio production are long gone. NBC launched a television station—KNBH, now KNBC—from this building in January 1949. The studio became obsolete in the era of color television, and KNBC moved to its new Burbank facilities in 1962; the building was demolished two years later. Today a banking giant, rather than a broadcast heavyweight, occupies the space. Wallichs Music City, on the northwest corner of Sunset and Vine, ran from 1940 to 1978. The first to have demonstration booths—where teenagers could listen to the latest vinyl 78s or 45s before buying—Wallichs was the world's largest specialty record store.

LEFT AND ABOVE: NBC opened its Art Deco–style studios at the northeast corner of Sunset Boulevard at Vine Street in 1938. This building replaced a 1927 facility in San Francisco that had managed the company's West Coast operations since its founding. In a reference to a nickname from its New York studio, NBC placed the words "Radio City" on the front of the building. Soon the area around the building was known as Radio City. Many radio studios and businesses sprang up, and radio was king of Hollywood—at least for a while. Hollywood's radio stations had the benefit of convenient access to stars like Bing Crosby, Jack Benny, and Bob Hope. CBS opened its studios a block away, and ABC set up shop a few doors north on Vine.

835— American Broadcasting Company (KECA), Vine Street, Hollywood, California

2C-H512

VINE STREET

The Hollywood Recreation Center has had many occupants through the years

ABOVE: The Broadway was a chain of department stores with branches across Southern California and its headquarters in Los Angeles. The first store was opened at 401 South Broadway in 1895. Englishman Arthur Letts bought the business in 1896 and expanded it by buying up his rivals. The large building at Fourth and Broadway became the flagship store, and at one point Letts owned both the Broadway and Bullocks Department Stores.

LEFT: In the 1920s, the motion picture and radio industries were blossoming and gravitated toward the office buildings newly constructed at Hollywood Boulevard and Vine Street. Just south of the intersection was the Hollywood Recreation Center, a 1935 Streamline Moderne building that originally housed bowling lanes, which Tom Breneman and Sammy Davis Jr. bought and leased to ABC Radio for their national broadcasts. Further along the street the Broadway sign sits atop what was originally the B. H. Dyas Specialty Emporium. Built in 1927 on the southwest corner of Hollywood and Vine, across from the Taft building, the Broadway Department Store took it over in 1931. Also south of Hollywood Boulevard, the Vine Street Theatre was built in 1926. During the 1930s this was the home of CBS Radio Playhouse, broadcasting the Lux Radio Theatre, which featured stars such as William Holden, Gloria Swanson, and George Raft.

ABOVE: Merv Griffin took over the ABC building at the end of the 1970s and renamed it the Celebrity Theater, home to the *Merv Griffin Show*. After the show ended its run, the building was vacated in 1993 and it became the home of transients who destroyed many of the historical details of the building, which suffered two suspicious fires. It was taken in hand and remodeled in 2004, with Hollywood Heritage keeping a close eye on the retention of the Streamline Moderne facade. The Broadway Department Store finally closed its doors in 1982, and although the historic sign remains, the buiding has been converted to apartments. After subsequent incarnations, the old CBS Radio Playhouse has become the Ricardo Montalbán Theatre.

1925

VIEW FROM VINE STREET
The nightclubs and radio studios have disappeared from Vine Street

LEFT: In 1925, when this photo was taken, Vine Street was lined with elegant restaurants such as the Brown Derby, Breneman's, and Al Levy's Tavern. Nightclubs like the Montmartre attracted stars such as Joan Crawford. Vine Street had beautiful speciality stores, as well as theaters that broadcast live radio shows with Jack Benny, George Burns, and others.

ABOVE: "It all changed after World War II," as locals say. People did not go dancing as much, tastes in theater changed, and so-called progress led to the modernization of many old establishments. Beautiful buildings were demolished, and restaurants were replaced by fast-food joints and drive-ins— which were then replaced by discount shops and thrift stores. Skyscrapers block the mountain views and the trolleys were replaced with newer, faster cars, but on a clear day one can still see the Hollywood sign.

1896

MASCAREL RANCH
Occupying the site that would become Gower Street above Hollywood Boulevard

78

LEFT: Photographed in 1896, Joe Mascarel's ranch was at Franklin and Gower. He was mayor of Los Angeles in 1865. Mascarel was a French sea captain who came here from Mexico in 1844. He married a Native American woman and became a successful merchant and property owner. Mascarel and his French partner bought valuable land in downtown Los Angeles and, in 1871, he cofounded the Farmers and Merchants Bank.

ABOVE: While the Farmers and Merchants Bank lives on downtown, all signs of the Mascarel Ranch are long gone. The area of Gower Street above Hollywood Boulevard near Franklin had become a residential area, but the beautiful homes, like so many others, have been torn down to make way for new streets, apartment buildings, cheap motels, commercial enterprises, and gas stations.

GLEN HOLLY HOTEL

For many years the springboard for investors looking to buy land in sunny California

1900

LEFT: The Glen Holly Hotel, popular in the late 1890s, was built a few years after the nearby Sackett Hotel, the first inn in the Cahuenga Valley. The Glen Holly Hotel had a country garden setting and was known for its beautiful roses. For tourists and prospective homeowners, tours of the area ran from this hotel. In 1900, when this photograph was taken, they advertised: "Pierce's Stage will drive you around the Cahuenga Valley and then back here for a Chicken Dinner—or as served—for 75 cents."

BELOW: The Glen Holly Hotel had stood on what is now the corner of Yucca and Ivar. It was replaced by elegant private homes, but like so much of old Hollywood, they were torn down in the 1960s and replaced with modern apartment buildings. Although these streets had become dilapidated in the 1980s, there is currently a gentrification effort afoot. The old Knickerbocker Hotel, just a few yards away from this site, is now a retirement home.

HOLLYWOOD BOULEVARD AT WILCOX AVENUE

Neither the Hurd House nor the surrounding fig and apricot trees survived the rise of Hollywood

LEFT: In 1887 the Los Angeles Ostrich Farm Railway Company built Hollywood's first railway, linking Dr. C. J. Sketchley's ostrich farm in Los Feliz with Hollywood. The Cahuenga Valley Railroad, installed in 1888, ran through the heart of the city and was called "the fast train to East Hollywood." This 1893 image shows the train on Hollywood at Wilcox Boulevard, in front of the Hurd House. The residents complained that "the engines caused great noise and frightened the horses," and so a long battle ensued.

BELOW: Wilcox Avenue was named for Daeida Wilcox who, along with her husband Harvey, bought an area of Rancho La Brea that they intended to call Figwood, but she later insisted that it be changed to Hollywood. Wilcox paved the main avenue, Prospect (now Hollywood Boulevard), and divided the land into tracts. The Hurd House was a Queen Anne–style house on the corner of Prospect and Wilcox and was bought by investor and developer H. J. Whitley in 1900. He would go on to develop Whitley Heights.

c.1900

ABOVE: Industrialist General Moses Sherman bought the Cahuenga Valley Railroad, which later became the Southern Pacific Railroad. Residents preferred horses or bicycles, but eventually warmed to the trains that took them as far as the ocean. Today the rail tracks are gone. In the 1970s, at the encouragement of the oil, tire, and automobile companies, all remaining train tracks were replaced by roads and freeways. Today this part of Hollywood is filled with small stores and vendors offering exotic clothing, discount gifts, and souvenirs.

EGYPTIAN THEATRE
Sid Grauman's first Hollywood movie house

BELOW AND RIGHT: The Egyptian Theatre, inspired by the discovery of King Tut's tomb, was the first Grauman theater in Hollywood, opening in 1922 with the premiere of Douglas Fairbanks's *Robin Hood*. It was the first theater to have a forecourt, and Grauman chose film props from the current movie for display. Four massive columns marked the entry, and on the roof, an actor in an Egyptian costume marched back and forth calling out the start to each performance. For Cecil B. DeMille's *The Ten Commandments* premiere in 1923, Grauman had over a hundred costumed performers on parade.

1932

BELOW: The Egyptian Theatre closed in 1992, and reopened in 1998 following a $15 million refurbishment. American Cinematheque (a nonprofit arts organization) bought it from the city for one dollar, promising to restore it to its former grandeur as a movie theater and add programs on filmmaking past and present. The historic ceilings and the 1922 theater organ were also repaired. Sharon Stone narrates the in-house documentary, "Forever Hollywood," and celebrity panels and historic tours are interspersed with screenings of old movies. The adjacent Pig 'n' Whistle Café (famous for its sundaes since 1927) was also restored and reopened.

LEFT: An obvious drawback to Grauman's Egyptian Theatre was a lack of a marquee to advertise its films to the passing public. This was added in Egyptian style and seen here in 1932, advertising the premiere of *Back Street*, starring Irene Dunne, John Boles, and Thelma Todd (see page 124).

EL CAPITAN THEATRE

The Walt Disney Company has returned the El Capitan to its former glory

LEFT: Real estate developer Charles Toberman (often dubbed the "Father of Hollywood") envisioned a thriving Hollywood theater district. Together with Sid Grauman, he built the Egyptian, El Capitan, and Chinese Theatres. The El Capitan opened on May 3, 1926, with *Charlot's Revue*, starring Jack Buchanan and Gertrude Lawrence. In the next decade, over 120 live plays were produced with luminaries such as Clark Gable and Joan Fontaine treading the boards. After the Great Depression, audiences declined and the El Capitan began to screen movies instead. It closed shortly after Orson Welles's *Citizen Kane* premiered there in 1941.

RIGHT AND BELOW: After a full conversion to a cinema, the theater reopened in 1942 as the Paramount. After the 1960s, the Paramount changed hands often. In 1989 the Walt Disney Company took over, restoring this historical gem to its original Spanish Colonial and East Indian splendor, adding a giant Wurlitzer theater organ and returning to its original name. Today, Disney films premiere at the El Capitan, along with live stage shows. Using the neighboring Masonic Temple (frequented by Charlie Chaplin, Bob Hope, and Cecil B. DeMille in its day), Disney has added attractions such as the Disney Monsters Fun Palace, Toy Story, a soda fountain, and the Studio Store. The El Capitan was used as the Muppets Theatre in *The Muppets* (2011). The *Jimmy Kimmel Live* show tapes next door. In 2014 the El Capitan screened a special "sing-along" return engagement of Disney's *Mary Poppins*, with the song lyrics projected onto the screen; patrons were encouraged to dress as their favorite character.

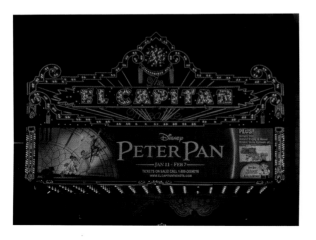

GRAUMAN'S CHINESE THEATRE

Sid Grauman's happy knack with publicity helped create the world's most famous cinema

BELOW: Grauman's Chinese Theatre opened on May 18, 1927. It was commissioned following the success of the nearby Grauman's Egyptian Theatre, which opened five years earlier. At a cost of $2 million, the theater was to be Sid Grauman's masterpiece. It opened with the premiere of Cecil B. DeMille's film *The King of Kings*. The opening attracted thousands of people, and the crowd became unruly as fans tried to catch a glimpse of arriving movie stars and celebrities. Grauman spared no expense on the theater's decor. He imported temple bells, pagodas, and other artifacts from China with special permission from the U.S. government. The first footprint ceremony took place on April 30, 1927, when Mary Pickford and Douglas Fairbanks pressed their feet into squares of wet cement. Norma Talmadge accidentally stepped into wet cement on the forecourt, giving showman Sid Grauman his famous idea.

RIGHT: Movie premieres at the Chinese Theatre could be elaborate affairs. Here World War I planes are strung out across the street for the 1930 premiere of the Howard Hughes film *Hell's Angels*, starring Jean Harlow.

c.1925

1930

BELOW: Known for its gala premieres, the Chinese Theatre had over 10,000 spectators for the 1939 opening of *The Wizard of Oz*. Ever since that sidewalk-shaping event in 1927, the stars of yesterday and today have left their footprints in the sidewalks near the theater. Little has changed at 6925 Hollywood Boulevard. Grauman's Chinese Theatre remains a much sought-after venue for premieres, and more than four million tourists visit its cement handprints and footprints in the forecourt every year. The theater is steeped in Hollywood tradition. The two original giant "Heaven Dogs" brought from China still guard the theater's entryway. Following the Northridge earthquake of 1994, an extensive retrofit was implemented. In 2013 the owners teamed with Chinese electronics manufacturer TCL (The Creative Life) in a 10-year, multimillion-dollar partnership that included naming rights. And so it is now officially known as the TCL Chinese Theatre until 2023.

ROOSEVELT HOTEL
Financed by the elite of Hollywood

ABOVE: A postcard advertising singer Elaine Dahl and Dan Roland and the Tunesmiths, a band familiar to the Los Angeles area. In 1940 Roland played at the Hollywood Plaza on Vine Street while Harold Ownes and His Royal Hawaiians played in the Roosevelt's Blossom Room.

LEFT: The Roosevelt Hotel was built in 1927, financed by a group of celebrities—including Douglas Fairbanks, Mary Pickford, and Louis B. Mayer—to house East Coast filmmakers and stars working in Hollywood. Clark Gable and Carole Lombard paid five dollars a night for their penthouse, Shirley Temple practiced tap dancing on the ornate tile stairs, Marilyn Monroe frequented the Cinegrill (which opened in 1936), Montgomery Clift stayed in room 928 while making *From Here to Eternity*, and the first Academy Awards ceremony was held here in the Blossom Room on May 16, 1929.

RIGHT: Today the spirits of both Marilyn Monroe and Montgomery Clift are said to haunt the hotel. Over the decades, guests have ranged from Frank Sinatra and Elizabeth Taylor to Lindsay Lohan and Paris Hilton. David Hockney recently renewed his original underwater mural in the pool next to the Tropicana poolside bar. The Roosevelt Hotel has been featured in many films, including *Beverly Hills Cop*, *Catch Me If You Can*, and *Charlie's Angels*.

c.1890

HOLLYWOOD CASH GROCERY

Hollywood's first general store

ABOVE: Built in 1886, the Hollywood Cash Grocery, the first permanent market and general merchandise store in Hollywood, was located on the northeast corner of Sunset and Cahuenga. Owner Alfred Watts hired a deliveryman who also picked up customers' mail on his route, then mailed it at the Prospect Park Post Office. Eventually, the government stopped him from "robbing" the local post office of business. Alfred Watts then bought another store on Edgemont Street.

c.1925

LEFT: The junction of Sunset and Cahuenga in the mid-1920s. Looking up the street, the tall building on the right-hand side is the Hollywood Athletic Club at 6525 Sunset Boulevard, which was completed in 1924. Membership cost $150, with monthly fees of $10.

BELOW: The days of such personal customer service seem to have vanished. This part of Hollywood no longer has the old mom-and-pop general stores; instead, many strip malls with chain stores have sprung up, each nearly indistinguishable from the next. This corner is now home to a Jack in the Box restaurant, which has undergone a major remodeling since 2002.

c.1925

PICKFORD STUDIOS

Jesse Hampton's original film studio is still a place where movies are made

ABOVE: Mary Pickford in *Rosita*, the film role that took her away from her previous roles as an ingenue.

BELOW: An aerial view of the *Robin Hood* film set shows the rate of development of the area in the 1920s when compared with the same view (left) a few years later.

LEFT: The set for the movie *The Thief of Baghdad* helps date this photograph to after 1924. This studio began as Hampton Studios when Jesse D. Hampton opened it to house his growing production company around 1918. Once Hampton moved to another locale, the "first couple" of Hollywood, Mary Pickford and Douglas Fairbanks, purchased the studio. In 1919, along with Charlie Chaplin and D. W. Griffith, Pickford and Fairbanks founded United Artists and used this studio as a base of operations. The studio released the classics *Robin Hood* (1922) and *The Thief of Baghdad*. The company added Howard Hughes, Walt Disney, and Samuel Goldwyn as independent producers, but still the business struggled.

ABOVE: Since the days of Fairbanks and Pickford, the studio has changed hands many times. During the 1950s, United Artists partner Samuel Goldwyn took over the facility, named it after himself, and generated hits such as *West Side Story* and *Some Like It Hot*. Warner Bros. purchased the studio in the 1980s and called it Warner Hollywood. Now featuring seven soundstages, the studio continues to be active, producing mostly television series. The studio was sold again in 1999 to BA Studios, a company that rents production facilities to Warner Bros. and other firms. Today the site is simply called "the Lot." Plans for the location include extensive renovations and the addition of an office tower.

c.1930

PARAMOUNT STUDIOS
The great Hollywood survivor

LEFT: Paramount is the only major film studio still operating in Hollywood. Famous Players-Lasky Corporation took over the 1917-built United Studios in 1926 and renamed it Paramount. Some of the biggest names in show business, including Mae West, W. C. Fields, and the Marx brothers, filmed here. In 1957 Desilu Productions (of the *I Love Lucy* series) took over RKO Studios on Gower, which eventually became part of the Paramount lot. The Bronson Gate, shown here, was featured in *Sunset Boulevard*, starring William Holden and Gloria Swanson.

RIGHT: In 1966 Paramount was taken over by Gulf and Western, which also absorbed Desilu Productions. Paramount then produced *Rear Window*, *Breakfast at Tiffany's*, and *The Godfather* trilogy. Paramount Television began in 1967 with series such as *Gunsmoke* and *Happy Days* and today has *Dr. Phil* and *Glee*. Viacom bought the studio in 1994 for $10 billion. The *Indiana Jones*, *Star Trek*, *Mission: Impossible*, *Anchorman*, and Jack Reacher movies are among some of Paramount's more recent successes.

RIGHT: The Paramount back lot has a seascape sky in front of a large water tank that, when empty, also doubles as a parking lot. It also has a variety of New York streets it can choose from.

c.1910

HOLLYWOOD MEMORIAL PARK / HOLLYWOOD FOREVER
Once again worthy of its glamorous Hollywood heritage

ABOVE: Established in 1899, the cemetery was founded by Isaac Van Nuys and was known as the Hollywood Memorial Park Cemetery. The cemetery was planned long before the movie business came to town, but today it is a Who's Who of old Hollywood. When Rudolph Valentino died in 1926 at the age of thirty-one, ten thousand people came to pay their respects. Mausoleums and elegant headstones in memory of stars such as Peter Finch, Jayne Mansfield, John Huston, Edward G. Robinson, Douglas Fairbanks, Cecil B. DeMille, Tyrone Power, Harrison Gray Otis, and Griffith J. Griffith are found here. Originally a hundred-acre park, the southern thirty-eight acres were sold to Paramount Studios.

BELOW: Jayne Mansfield gets a simple granite marker, while Douglas Fairbanks and son Douglas Fairbanks Jr. have a grand monument and reflecting pool in their memory.

ABOVE: The cemetery was renamed Hollywood Forever when Tyler and Brent Cassity bought it for $375,000 in 1998. It had fallen into decline from the 1940s after being bought by fraudster Jules Roth, who had asset-stripped the business. The 1994 Northridge earthquake had toppled headstones and damaged roads, and maintenance and restoration was sorely needed. The Cassity family brought a new energy to a neglected cemetery park. They added a Day of the Dead celebration, weddings, and silent-movie nights in the summer with picnics and movies projected on mausoleum walls. Around 3,000 attend the regular music concerts. For families of the "residents," a Life Stories service is highly popular: either written or video memoirs are available—including Life Stories of the celebrities buried there. Actress Joan Hackett still makes people smile—her gravestone reads: "Go away, I'm sleeping." The ghost of actor Clifton Webb is said to haunt his mausoleum in the park. One of the more recent interments—Johnny Ramone in 2004—has generated its own annual tribute with contemporaries of the Ramones' guitarist putting in appearances.

1973

WHISKY A GO GO
Where a generation of rock acts paid their dues

1964

LEFT: On January 15, 1964, Elmer Valentine introduced Whisky a Go Go to an unsuspecting world and changed the music scene forever. Singer-songwriter-guitarist Johnny Rivers became an instant success when he performed live at the discotheque that night. In between sets, female DJs played music for the crowd to dance to, suspended in a glass cage above the stage, simply because there was not enough floor room. In the glass cage, the Go Go girls in their fringed minidresses and white boots created an indelible image. Johnny Rivers's career skyrocketed. An eclectic group of bands found a home on the Sunset Strip at the Whisky, including the Byrds, Alice Cooper, Van Morrison, the Mamas and the Papas, Frank Zappa, Janis Joplin, Otis Redding, Smokey Robinson, the Four Tops, and Jimi Hendrix.

ABOVE: George Harrison reacts angrily to the presence of press photographers as the Beatles drop in at Whisky a Go Go in 1964. Ringo Starr is to his left and John Lennon is to his right, at the edge of the frame.

ABOVE: Through the decades, musicians from all spheres have found an audience here. The Whisky was instrumental in bringing punk and new wave to audiences on the West Coast. In turn, it hosted heavy metal and the grunge movement, with Mudhoney, Soundgarden, and Hole playing at the Whisky. Meanwhile, new Whisky a Go Go nightclubs opened up all over the world. Black Sabbath announced their reunion at the original Whisky in 2011. On January 16, 2014, Whisky a Go Go celebrated its fiftieth birthday on the Sunset Strip, commemorating five decades as a major part of Los Angeles nightlife.

c.1938

CROSSROADS OF THE WORLD

A striking development from the pen of Robert V. Derrah

LEFT: Once called "L.A.'s first modern shopping mall," Crossroads of the World opened in 1936 on Sunset Boulevard, near Las Palmas. Boris Karloff, Cesar Romero, and Binnie Barnes were among the celebrities at the opening. The unique center building resembles a ship, complete with portholes and decks, as well as a thirty-foot tower topped by a revolving world globe. The bungalows surrounding this are a mixture of Italian, Spanish, French, and New England designs from architect Robert V. Derrah. This quaint pedestrian precinct with stylish boutiques was very popular from the 1930s through the 1960s. Songwriter Jimmy Webb had an office here, as did Liberace's elder brother, George Liberace.

ABOVE AND LEFT: The boutiques in Crossroads of the World have been replaced by small businesses and TV casting offices. The Hollywood Arts Council office is on the top deck. Crossroads has often been featured in films: as Demi Moore's office in *Indecent Proposal*, Danny DeVito's office in *L.A. Confidential*, and in commercials and music videos. The Church of the Blessed Sacrament is visible to the right.

c.1940

SCHWAB'S PHARMACY

Where Hollywood bought its drugs and sodas

LEFT: Despite the stories, Lana Turner was not discovered at Schwab's Pharmacy on Sunset and Crescent Heights, but Marlene Dietrich, the Marx brothers, and Charles Laughton were regulars. Harold Arlen wrote "Somewhere Over the Rainbow" in a booth at Schwab's in 1939, William Holden hung out here in *Sunset Boulevard*, and Brigitte Bardot bought European toilet paper here. This was not just an ordinary drugstore—Schwab's sold top-quality cosmetics and the best ice-cream sodas, and attracted the likes of James Dean and Dick Powell.

BELOW: Starlet Angela Lansbury photographed in Schwab's around the time she was nominated for Best Supporting Actress for her role in *The Picture of Dorian Gray*. MGM had signed her up as a teenager. She was also nominated for an Oscar for her first film, *Gaslight* (1944).

1945

ABOVE: Right up until it closed in 1986, agents, managers, and talent scouts discussed business in Schwab's booths. Shelley Winters held court every morning, and Cher, Linda Ronstadt, and Sally Kellerman were regulars. Sadly, despite promises to preserve it, Schwab's was torn down in 1988.

Today it has been replaced by a multistory complex: the Virgin Megastore is gone, but there are movie theaters, Trader Joe's, Crunch Gym, Starbucks, and restaurants that attract young celebrities and the hip and trendy crowds.

1911

LA BREA TAR PITS
Repository of a wide variety of pre–Ice Age flora and fauna

ABOVE: Fossil miners work at the La Brea Tar Pits in this 1911 photograph. At Rancho La Brea, tar (*brea* in Spanish) has been seeping up for thousands of years. Over the centuries, animals attracted by the surface water fell in, sank in the tar, and their bones were preserved. Humans found uses for the tar early on; Native Americans discovered the use of the tar for waterproofing purposes. Spanish explorers and settlers used the natural source of asphalt to caulk their ships and create waterproof roofing of early adobes. Around 1900, a worldwide fascination with dinosaurs, fossils, and anthropology emerged, but it wasn't until after World War II that new technologies made it possible for many more artifacts to be uncovered from the black depths of La Brea. A great number of large mammal skeletons were found, as well as the partial skeleton of a woman thought to date back 9,000 years.

ABOVE: Fossils of the dire wolf, saber-toothed tiger, woolly mammoth, short-faced bear, and ground sloth have been found in the La Brea Tar Pits, in enough quantities to keep researchers busy well into the next century. The George C. Page Museum on the site is dedicated to researching the tar pits and displaying specimens from the animals that have been found there. Page built the museum from the fortune he made shipping oranges to places like his home state of Nebraska. The museum displays the largest and most diverse collection of extinct Ice Age plants and animals in the world. Through windows at the Page Museum Laboratory, visitors watch specialists clean and repair specimens. Outside, in Hancock Park, life-size replicas of several extinct mammals are featured. Once a year, visitors can view volunteers excavating the pits under the supervision of paleontologists.

c.1940

BEVERLY HILLS HOTEL
When it opened, it was a countryside retreat

LEFT: The Beverly Hills Hotel was built in 1912 by developer Burton Green on twelve acres of farmland. Beverly Hills had been named after President Taft's Beverly Farm in Massachusetts. Stars John Barrymore, W. C. Fields, Will Rogers, and Charlie Chaplin were early visitors to the restaurants, especially the Polo Lounge. In the 1940s, it was repainted pink and green, resulting in the nickname "the Pink Palace." Howard Hughes rented bungalows there for thirty years and Johnny Weissmuller, Joan Crawford, and Katharine Hepburn swam in the famous pool.

BELOW: The extensive grounds of the Beverly Hills Hotel when it first opened.

c.1915

ABOVE: Previously a favorite with stars like Elizabeth Taylor, Frank Sinatra, Spencer Tracy, and John Lennon, the famous Polo Lounge is still a popular meeting place for stars, Hollywood big shots, and award-show parties. The Beverly Hills Hotel (which was once owned by Irene Dunne and Loretta Young) was bought in 1987 by the sultan of Brunei for $187 million. Since then, over $100 million has been spent on renovations while maintaining the site's historical integrity, under the care of the Dorchester Collection management. Having commemorated the hotel's hundredth anniversary in 2012, another facelift was then launched. The lobby, Polo Lounge, pool area, and guest rooms were transformed in time for the yearlong celebrations for the City of Beverly Hills' centennial in 2014.

c.1931

BEVERLY HILLS CITY HALL

The Beverly Hills City Hall is a complete contrast to that of Los Angeles

LEFT: In 1906 Burton Green formed the Rodeo Land and Water Company and planned a new, luxurious city, calling it Beverly Hills. It had previously been just a small train stop, called Morocco, on the route through the bean fields down to the ocean. The land was later sold for oil development. In 1919 Mary Pickford and Douglas Fairbanks built their famous home, Pickfair, and launched the migration of motion-picture people to the area. The Beverly Hills City Hall, as seen here, was built in 1931 in a bean field. Designed by architect William Gage in the Spanish Renaissance style, the building opened in 1932. After fifty years of service, it was extensively cleaned and restored in 1982.

ABOVE: Carefully planned, the city has strict zoning laws. While stars of Hollywood's golden age—such as Elizabeth Taylor, Gene Kelly, Jimmy Stewart, Kirk Douglas, and George Burns—used to live in Beverly Hills, many of today's residents are the foreign-born wealthy. The Beverly Hills Civic Center, designed by Charles Moore in 1988, links the new library and the police and fire departments with the historic Spanish-style city hall at 455 North Rexford Drive. It was restored in 1992. The governors of this city hall coordinated the many commemorative activities for the 2014 yearlong City of Beverly Hills centennial.

BEVERLY WILSHIRE HOTEL

The Beverly Hills Speedway made way for this grand hotel

c.1935

c.1913

LEFT: In the 1920s, the Beverly Hills Speedway was always packed with spectators, including celebrities like Wallace Beery, Charlie Chaplin, and Tom Mix. The autodrome closed in 1924 when some of the land (between Wilshire Boulevard and Pico, from Beverly Drive to Lasky) was needed to create the swank Beverly Wilshire Hotel. Built in 1927 by the Courtright family, the elegant hotel was an immediate success. Over the years, Dashiell Hammett wrote *The Thin Man* at the Wilshire, Cary Grant and Elvis Presley were residents, and Steve McQueen kept his motorcycles on site.

BELOW: The hotel is where Rodeo Drive now meets Wilshire Boulevard. John Lennon stayed here, and Warren Beatty and Elvis Presley both rented the penthouse. Michael Caine, Anthony Hopkins, and other stars, politicians, and royalty are frequent visitors. Julia Roberts and Richard Gere stayed here in *Pretty Woman*—as did Eddie Murphy in *Beverly Hills Cop*. Hernando Courtright sold the hotel in 1985, when it became the Regent Beverly Wilshire Hotel. Since 1998, it has been managed by the Four Seasons Hotel group, which spent $35 million to renovate the building. In 2006 the hotel became the Beverly Wilshire, a Four Seasons hotel. It was listed on the National Register of Historic Places in 1987.

c.1940

CHURCH OF THE GOOD SHEPHERD
Witness to many star-studded weddings and funerals

LEFT: It's hard to believe that this beautiful edifice started out as a wooden hut in the midst of lima bean fields. The congregation grew and, with generous donations, the present Church of the Good Shepherd was built on Santa Monica Boulevard in 1923. Early parishioners included Bing Crosby and Rudolph Valentino, whose funeral service was held here in 1926. The funerals of Rita Hayworth and Alfred Hitchcock were also at the Good Shepherd.

1950

LEFT: Elizabeth Taylor was just eighteen years old when she married twenty-three-year-old hotel heir Conrad "Nicky" Hilton at the Good Shepherd. The marriage was said to be in trouble just fourteen weeks into their European honeymoon.

ABOVE: In 1950 Elizabeth Taylor married Conrad Hilton here. Other celebrity weddings included Rod Stewart to Rachel Hunter, and Mark Wahlberg to Rhea Durham. Today this beautiful "small house of worship" and local parish church seems untouched by time. In 1998 the world watched the funeral of Frank Sinatra here. Stars in attendance included Gregory Peck, Sidney Poitier, Jack Lemmon, Liza Minnelli, Kirk Douglas, and Debbie Reynolds.

c.1925

WITCH'S HOUSE
Ding-dong, the Witch's House lives on

ABOVE: This whimsical "storybook" house was built in 1921 as the Willat Studios on Washington Boulevard in Culver City. It appeared in several of their silent movies. The designer, Harry C. Oliver, won an Academy Award for Art Direction on the 1927 film *Seventh Heaven*. Carl A. Willat (one of the developers of Technicolor) and his brother Irvin Willat then sold the studios to producer Ward Lascelle who, because of traffic problems caused by gawkers, moved the Witch's House to a quiet street in Beverly Hills.

116

ABOVE: It was converted to a private residence, and subsequent owners included Louis Spadina and Martin and Doris Green, who moved away in 1987. Abandoned, the property fell into neglect. In 1998 realtor Michael Libow bought the Witch's House for $1.3 million, saving it from destruction and promising to preserve this historical icon, which has three bedrooms, as well as a loft and a moat. After a complete restoration, the City of Beverly Hills declared the Witch's House a cultural landmark, protecting it from future demolition. The site was featured in the 1965 Rod Steiger movie *The Loved One* and later in *Clueless* starring Alicia Silverstone.

c.1925

BEL AIR GATES

Home to the substantially rich and the substantially famous

118

LEFT: Founded in the 1920s by oil millionaire turned developer Alphonso Bell, the residential area of Bel Air hides behind magnificent Spanish gates on Sunset Boulevard near UCLA and is protected by the Bel Air Patrol. Equally hidden, down the winding roads, is the famous Bel Air Hotel. A discreet oasis for the rich and famous, this picturesque 1922-built, Mission-style property was originally a real-estate office and riding stables. The hotel opened in 1946. The Rockefellers, Kennedys, and Howard Hughes were regular patrons. Privacy-seeking stars such as Greta Garbo, Marion Davies, Gary Cooper, Audrey Hepburn, Grace Kelly, and Sophia Loren found solace in the secluded lush and leafy grounds.

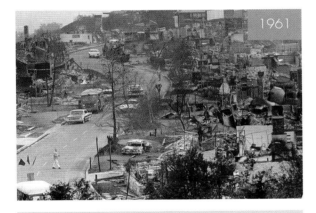

1961

THE BEL AIR FIRE

Winds of up to fifty-one miles per hour fanned a fire that began on the north slope of the Santa Monica Mountains on November 6, 1961. The windstorm blew flames that raced through tinder-dry vegetation across Mulholland Drive and down the south slope into Stone Canyon. Intense heat and the high-velocity winds it created pushed the fire around and through natural and man-made barriers. In the end, the flames consumed 484 homes and twenty-one other buildings. J. R. Eyerman of Time-Life Pictures snapped photographs of the devastation.

ABOVE: Bel Air is still an enclave of opulent homes that seem more like palaces, with servants' quarters, stables, guesthouses, tennis courts, and spacious gardens. No shops are allowed within the hallowed Bel Air gates: the Bel Air Hotel is the only commercial property permitted. It is now owned by the sultan of Brunei, who closed it for two years and spent $100 million on renovations, reopening it in 2011. The classic TV series *The*

Beverly Hillbillies filmed here, as did *The Rockford Files* and *Get Shorty*. But normally such intrusions are forbidden. Among the illustrious longtime residents were Ronald Reagan, Elizabeth Taylor, Alfred Hitchcock, Johnny Carson, and mogul Kirk Kerkorian. Today those who call Bel Air home include Kim Kardashian and Kanye West.

c.1932

HELMS BAKERY

For thirty-eight years the Helms vans were "daily at your door"

ABOVE: In 1926 New Yorker Paul Helms moved his family to Southern California for health reasons. By 1931 Helms had constructed and opened Helms Bakery on Venice Boulevard in Culver City, with thirty-two employees and eleven delivery vans. The following year, Helms Bakery became the official baker for the 1932 Olympics. Through the 1930s, 1940s, and 1950s, over 500 Helms "coaches" delivered bread and pastries daily to homes across Los Angeles; their products were never sold in shops. In the unique Helms yellow-and-blue vans, the uniformed

Helmsman would sound the distinct "toot-toot" whistle to signal his arrival in the neighborhood. "Daily at your door" was the motto. Customers would run out to the vans for fresh Olympic bread and to see what fresh-baked treats were displayed in the long wooden trays: doughnuts, brownies, cupcakes, cookies, and assorted pastries.

RIGHT: A fleet of bread coaches outside the Art Deco bakery on Venice Boulevard. A statue of the Helmsman stood at the entrance, and after the factory closed it was moved to Burton W. Chace Park overlooking Marina Del Rey Harbor.

c.1940

ABOVE: The iconic yellow-and-blue vans from the Olympic baker. Customers could view the bread, cakes, and pastries in the long wooden trays that slid out from the rear.

ABOVE: This tradition carried on for almost forty years, until the cost of sending out these vans became prohibitive and supermarkets were sprouting up, stocking less expensive bread. The Helmsmen stopped calling in 1969, and Helms Bakery closed. The Helms building was purchased in 1974 by Walter N. Marks, another family businessman and philanthropist like Paul Helms. Carefully restored as a "pop art icon," the Helms Bakery District opened in 2013. Managed by Walter Marks's company, the property is filled with artisans, antique shops, vintage clothing boutiques, the Jazz Bakery, furniture stores, new eateries—and a Helms Museum. The facility is partially powered by solar energy. A Helms Bakery Collectors Club was formed for those nostalgic for the sound of that "toot-toot" whistle and the yellow-and-blue vans.

c.1975

MERLE NORMAN BUILDING
Part of the city's rich Streamline Moderne architectural heritage

c.1967

ABOVE AND BELOW: Architect Robert V. Derrah launched a smaller ship with his Crossroads of the World building (see page 100) in 1936. It proved to be the forerunner to a fully blown ocean liner, the magnificent Coca-Cola Building of 1939. The Coca-Cola Building still bottles soda, although it now has the distinction of doing it in a designated Los Angeles Historic-Cultural Monument.

LEFT: Founded in 1931, the Merle Norman cosmetics company thrived on the motto "Try before you buy." Norman's business was doing well enough for her to move into this beautiful Streamline Moderne–adapted building in 1936 to use as headquarters. Architect Jack Parker added Streamline Moderne (an offshoot of the Art Deco movement) elements to an extant building. Typical Streamline Moderne elements were complex curves and pylons, giving the look of an abstract ocean liner.

ABOVE: The building was acquired from Merle Norman by E. M. Stolaroff in 1961 and today has multiple tenants. The Streamline Moderne beauty looks even better today, especially during the holidays when strings of lights adorn the "abstract ocean liner" main mast. Merle Norman's corporate business is run from an office near Los Angeles International Airport, and they continue to offer franchises to would-be cosmetics salespeople. It was designated a Santa Monica landmark in 2002.

1929

UCLA
The University of California, Los Angeles, has never stopped growing

LEFT: The University of California, Los Angeles (UCLA), seen here in 1929, is a public university founded in 1919. The school grew so fast that just a decade after its founding, it needed a larger campus. The new campus was undergoing construction in 1929, the year of this photograph. Architects designed all five campus buildings in the Romanesque Revival style. The first class to graduate at the new Westwood campus had 5,500 students. The first master's degrees were awarded in 1933, and the first doctorate in 1936. Royce Hall, with its pair of steeples, is seen at left center of the main photo; the domed Powell Library sits across from it. Haines Hall and Kinsey Hall are behind them, on the left and right respectively.

ABOVE: A modern view of Royce Hall seen from the top left corner of both the archive and modern aerial pictures. The school boasts more applicants than any university in the nation.

ABOVE: One nickname for UCLA is "Under Construction Like Always." The student population continues to grow, and construction and renovation projects are nearly continuous. Royce Hall and the Powell Library still anchor the heart of the campus. Currently underway are expansions of the life sciences and engineering research complexes. With its 8.2 million volumes, the UCLA library system stands among the top ten libraries in the United States. With just four buildings at its onset, the campus now has 163 buildings to serve its student body. Campus amenities include sculpture gardens, fountains, museums, and, a mile from campus in Bel Air, a Japanese garden.

c.1925

MGM-SONY STUDIOS
"Do it right, do it big, give it class"

ABOVE AND RIGHT: Founded in 1924 under Louis B. Mayer's guidance, Metro-Goldwyn-Mayer Studios was best known for musicals such as *The Wizard of Oz*, *Singin' in the Rain*, and the Fred Astaire–Ginger Rogers films. MGM's stable of stars included Judy Garland, Mickey Rooney, Elizabeth Taylor, Gene Kelly, and Spencer Tracy. The original main gate was on Washington Boulevard in Culver City. MGM Studios covered more than 180 acres of land and was divided into six working studio complexes, known as "lots." At the front of the studios, Lot One was the (Irving) Thalberg Building, housing the production, casting, and other administration offices. Also on this lot were makeup and hairdressing, special effects, film-processing laboratories, publicity, a commissary, and a barbershop. MGM had twenty-eight soundstages. Stage 27 served as "Munchkinland" in *The Wizard of Oz*. Epics such as *Mutiny on the Bounty*, *Ben Hur*, and others were filmed on the vast backlots.

126

c.1925

ABOVE: Like many studios that caught a financial chill from the postwar preference for television, MGM started to lose money and their extensive production facilities—which had once been their major asset—now became an unsustainable overhead. The old company motto of "Do it right, do it big, give it class" had to be set aside. The company began selling off back lots to be converted into real-estate tracts. MGM merged with United Artists in 1980 and then sold their famous studios to Lorimar Television. In 1990

Sony Entertainment took over what remained of the old MGM lot. Once the owners of the largest, most glamorous studio, MGM is now run from offices in Beverly Hills. Sony spent $100 million renovating the former MGM lot, which now has one of the best postproduction facilities. The film and television studio complex is home to long-running game shows *Jeopardy!* and *Wheel of Fortune*.

THELMA TODD'S CAFÉ

Thelma Todd was a femme fatale who lived up to her billing

LEFT: Thelma Todd was an actress in the Jean Harlow mold. In the 1930s, she appeared in several Marx brothers comedies, including *Horse Feathers* and *Monkey Business*. She also ran Thelma Todd's Café, which overlooked the ocean at 17575 Pacific Coast Highway between Malibu and Pacific Palisades. In 1935 she was found dead in her car in the garage of former silent movie star Jewel Carmen. The police investigation ruled her death an "accidental suicide" from carbon monoxide poisoning, but the puzzling aspect was that she had a bloodied lip. There were no other marks of a violent struggle, but Todd did not leave a suicide note. The investigation suggested that Todd heated up the car in the confines of the garage and was overcome by the fumes. A cover-up was suspected, but the mystery was never solved. The Chez Roland Beach Club later took over through 1950.

c.1932

ABOVE: Screen star Thelma Todd was just twenty-nine when she died under mysterious circumstances. Her death has never been properly explained.

BELOW: After years of neglect, the Mediterranean Revival–style building was bought by Paulist Productions. Founded by Father Elwood Kaiser in 1968 and dedicated to producing "uplifting entertainment that unifies the human family," they use the best actors—such as Ted Danson, Martin Sheen, and Ally Sheedy—writers, and directors, who are happy to work for minimum pay. Mostly shown on the TNT and Hallmark cable channels, Paulist produced the *Insight* series and has been working on the true story of Home Boy Industries, a gang recovery program. In 2002 the entire property was renovated. Employees in the production offices claim to have seen Thelma Todd's ghost walking down the stairs.

c. 1905

ST. MARK'S HOTEL
Developer Abbot Kinney wanted to capitalize on the cachet of Venice

c.1910

LEFT: In 1904 entrepreneur Abbot Kinney established a beachfront theme park called Venice of America. Architect Norman E. March emulated Venice, Italy, when designing this new area, which drew crowds to the ocean. On July 4, 1905, Kinney invited thousands of potential buyers to Venice's grand opening. The centerpiece was the elegant, columned St. Mark's Hotel. Catering to the rich and famous, St. Mark's welcomed stars such as Charlie Chaplin, Sarah Bernhardt, Theda Bara, and Douglas Fairbanks, who also enjoyed the Venice Casino and Dance Pavilion.

BELOW: The Depression of the 1930s took its toll on Venice, and eventually the St. Mark's Hotel was abandoned. By the 1970s, many of the beautiful Italianate buildings had crumbled or were demolished, and the arched windows were filled in or modernized. The original Hotel St. Mark has disappeared, but the building seen here is one of the few reminders of Windward Avenue's rich architectural past. Since the late 1990s, architects and New Agers have rediscovered this historical resort and have been restoring the area. The old building took the name St. Mark's for a while, but is now a popular eclectic eatery called Danny's.

1925

VENICE PIER

Kinney's big drawer owed more to Coney Island than to anything in the Venice lagoon

c.1910

LEFT: Abbot Kinney used his tobacco millions to buy two miles of oceanfront real estate. He hoped to turn the marshy land at the property's southern end into a resort as impressive as Venice, Italy. He dug miles of canals and drained the marshes so he could offer building sites on dry land, but that was just the start. The main attraction was the 1,200-foot-long Kinney Pier, seen here in this 1925 photograph. It was already the second pier on the site, as the first burned in 1920. It was chock-full of amusements, an auditorium, a restaurant, a dance hall, and a hot saltwater plunge. The town had a block-long arcaded business street with Venetian architecture and a miniature railroad. Kinney's town had more than 3,000 residents after just five years and grew to 10,000 soon after. On some weekends, an estimated 150,000 tourists visited. He ruled his town with an iron fist until his death in 1920.

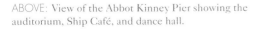

ABOVE: View of the Abbot Kinney Pier showing the auditorium, Ship Café, and dance hall.

ABOVE: Sand on the shoreline seems to point the way to the site of Abbot Kinney's long-disappeared pier. Los Angeles annexed Venice Beach five years after Kinney's death, and closed the pier as soon as the lease ran out. By 1929 the majority of the canals had been paved over. Discovery of oil nearby added to the decay of the place as a resort. Today, the few remaining canals set Venice Beach apart, and the circuslike Ocean Front Walk continues a spirit of amusement. Walking, bicycling, and working out at the famed Muscle Beach are popular activities at the seafront. Muscle Beach is famous for its beachside weight pen, which has been frequented by notable bodybuilders such as Arnold Schwarzenegger. Venice is where Jim Morrison met Ray Manzarek to form the Doors. An endless series of movie scenes have been shot here, starting with Charlie Chaplin's *Kid Auto Races at Venice* and *The Circus*, all the way to *Million Dollar Baby*.

c.1910

VIEW FROM WINDWARD AVENUE

Today's visitors to Windward Avenue are more likely to stroll down the street than ride a train

LEFT: When this photo was taken in 1910, Windward Avenue was the hub of excitement at Venice Beach. Abbot Kinney had introduced Coney Island–style roller coasters, dance halls, the Venice Plunge (a pseudo-Arabian bathhouse), and camel rides at the Streets of Cairo attraction. Miniature train rides, arcades, and carnival shows were among the attractions that people came to Venice to enjoy—and some preferred a simple stroll through the colonnades in the sea air and sunshine.

ABOVE: At the ocean, Windward Avenue is now lined with the remnants of beautiful buildings. In 2006 the Venice Historical Society enlisted the support of writer Ray Bradbury to raise money to save and restore the old structures. When Bradbury lived in Venice, he wrote *The Foghorn*. Today, secondhand shops, boutiques, and small art galleries nestle in with taco stands, juice bars, and coffee shops. Musicians, street performers, and skateboarders abound. The Venice Boardwalk is world-famous. The annual Hare Krishna parade is held here, and this colorful area has been featured in *Baywatch*. Small, two-bedroom homes here now cost more than $1 million.

c.1935

VENICE CANAL

A problem with drainage and eroding concrete spoiled Kinney's grand canal vision

ABOVE: In 1904, when Abbot Kinney was building Venice, he envisioned a fleet of Venetian gondoliers poling their way through interconnecting canals. Sixteen miles of canals were dug from salt marshes, bungalows were built alongside them, and people took to their boats and enjoyed water carnivals.

Unfortunately, the canals were cheaply constructed with unreinforced concrete and soon the banks began to erode. Water started to undermine the sidewalks and the canals were steadily filled with pollution, sediment, and rubble. In 1942 the majority were withdrawn from public use and paved over.

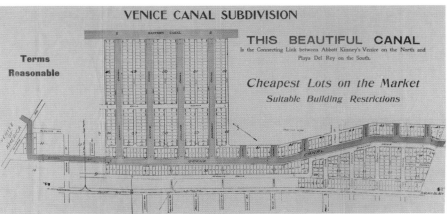

VENICE CANAL SUBDIVISION

THIS BEAUTIFUL CANAL

Is the Connecting Link between Abbott Kinney's Venice on the North and Playa Del Rey on the South.

Terms Reasonable

Cheapest Lots on the Market

Suitable Building Restrictions

ABOVE: Artists and hippies loved living here, and Jim Morrison of the Doors called the area home during the 1960s. The Grand Canal, at Windward and Main, where all the waterways connected, has long been paved over. In the 1980s, as real-estate prices soared, the bohemian canal-dwellers were replaced by the wealthy. In 1994 the city finally refurbished the six remaining canals. Still a magnet for artists and filmmakers, the canals—with a myriad of quaint bridges—run through a picturesque and tranquil neighborhood.

LEFT: Kinney had incorporated his landholding as the City of Ocean Park in 1904 (it became the City of Venice in 1911 and part of Los Angeles in 1925). The Venice canal subdivision was to the south of his original Ocean Park development.

c.1940

SANTA MONICA PIER
Still a popular destination for show-goers, anglers, and thrill-seekers

LEFT: The first local Santa Monica pier was built in 1874 at Shoo-Fly Landing, as a loading point for tar from the inland La Brea Tar Pits. It was removed in 1879, and the current Santa Monica Pier was later built to the north. Originally two adjoining piers, the longer 1909 Municipal Pier (to carry sewage out to sea) and the shorter 1916 Looff Pleasure Pier, were strictly for entertainment and anglers. With frequent storm damage and endless renovations, the two were consolidated as the Santa Monica Pier. In 1922, on the Pleasure Pier side, a merry-go-round was installed; it became a classic. The forty-four wooden horses the children rode were hand-carved by a New York furniture maker, Charles Looff, the pier's owner. The iconic carousel was housed in the Byzantine-styled hippodrome Looff had built in 1916.

ABOVE AND LEFT: By the late 1960s, many attractions had disappeared; the Santa Monica Pier was in trouble. Listed on the National Register of Historic Places, the pier and the carousel became famous when featured in movies such as *The Sting* with Robert Redford and Paul Newman. When the Santa Monica Pier fell into disrepair in the 1970s, the carousel was threatened with destruction. But many people with fond memories fought to preserve it. In 1983 terrible rainstorms washed away part of the pier. Now the pier has been rebuilt and is heavily visited once more. The restored 1917 Billiard's Building is now home of Rusty's Surf Ranch, with vintage surfing memorabilia and billiards tournaments. Tony Award winner Paul Sand runs the new West End Theatre above the Mariasol restaurant. Le Cirque du Soleil's big top is set up each year in their trademark blue-and-yellow tents, seating 2,600 people, next to the pier. However, the Twilight Concert series in the summer has become so successful that the local city council wants to scale them down because of public safety issues. The Santa Monica Pier Aquarium is below the eastern deck. The adjoining Pacific Amusement Park, which opened in 1996, has the world's first solar-powered Ferris wheel. And there's always fishing at the end of the pier.

LIFE BOAT

ARTHUR BARD & CO.
BUILDERS & CONTRACTORS
M.A. BARD, GENERAL MANAGER
PHONE TRINITY 5058. UNION OIL BLDG. LOS ANGELES, CAL.
CLUB CASA DEL MAR

Club Casa Del Mar

BARKER BROS.

1926

140

HOTEL CASA DEL MAR

The rise, fall, and rise again of a "grand dame"

LEFT: Casa Del Mar opened in 1926 as a beach club in Santa Monica. Designed by Charles F. Plummer, the Renaissance Revival–style club with hand-painted ceilings and bronze statuary was the classiest building in Santa Monica. The social elite and Hollywood celebrities flocked to the hotel. During World War II, Casa Del Mar became a military hotel, reverting to a public hotel when the war was over. In the 1960s, the building housed the controversial Synanon drug rehab program. From 1978 until 1997, the Pritikin Longevity Center was headquartered here.

BELOW: It was then bought by the Edward Thomas Hospitality Corporation, owners of the adjacent Shutters on the Beach Hotel. In October 1999, the Hotel Casa Del Mar reopened, seventy-five years after its debut. More than $50 million was spent on the restoration of this historic landmark, giving this grand dame a 1920s feel. The grand ballroom has Venetian glass chandeliers, the gardens are landscaped, and a new health club and business center have been added.

c.1920

VIEW OF SANTA MONICA BEACH
A resort since 1875

ABOVE: Founded in 1875, Santa Monica was a popular seaside resort town. Ornate bathhouses were built where visitors changed into their swimsuits, and bathing-beauty contests were held on the beach. Movie stars and the wealthy built summer homes here. The boardwalks reached from the Venice Pier to the Santa Monica Pier, and others sprang up in between, including the Pickering Pier, Rosemary Pier, Lick Pier, and Fraser's Million Dollar Pier, which burned in 1912.

RIGHT: The first bathing-beauty contest was sponsored by the *Los Angeles Examiner* in 1912. They became a regular feature in Venice, Santa Monica, and Long Beach.

c.1920

ABOVE: In the 1970s, the remaining bathhouses were demolished. The fancy oceanside homes remain, although in recent years some have been lost to high-tide damage and floods. As the years passed, many of the piers crumbled or—because they were all wooden—burned down. Only the Santa Monica Pier survives, along with its iconic nine-story Pacific Wheel, the only Ferris wheel in California situated over the ocean. Today, Los Angelenos and tourists flock to the beach, inline skaters and skateboarders fill the boardwalk, and surfers and swimmers enjoy the waves and breathtaking sunsets.